Build It Once

A Basic Primer for the Creation of Online Exhibitions

Sarah Goodwin Thiel

The Scarecrow Pr
Lanham, Maryland • Toron
2007

SCARECROW PRESS, INC.

Published in the United States of America
by Scarecrow Press, Inc.
A wholly owned subsidiary of
The Rowman & Littlefield Publishing Group, Inc.
4501 Forbes Boulevard, Suite 200, Lanham, Maryland 20706
www.scarecrowpress.com

Estover Road
Plymouth PL6 7PY
United Kingdom

British Library Cataloguing in Publication Information Available

Library of Congress Cataloging-in-Publication Data

Thiel, Sarah Goodwin, 1957–
  Build it once : a basic primer for the creation of online exhibitions / Sarah
Goodwin Thiel.
     p. cm.
  Includes bibliographical references and index.
  ISBN-13: 978-0-8108-5225-9 (pbk. : alk. paper)
  ISBN-10: 0-8108-5225-X (pbk. : alk. paper)
  1. Library exhibits—Computer network resources. 2. Museum exhibits—
Computer network resources. 3. Web sites—Design. I. Title.

Z717.T54 2007
021.70285—dc22   2006035338

⊖™ The paper used in this publication meets the minimum requirements of
American National Standard for Information Sciences—Permanence of
Paper for Printed Library Materials, ANSI/NISO Z39.48-1992.
Manufactured in the United States of America.

Contents

Acknowledgments

My special thanks go to Brian Baird, former Preservation Officer of the University of Kansas Libraries, for encouraging me to write this book; Mary Howe, Lawrence, KS independent instructional designer, for sharing her technical expertise and generous support; John Brewer, Lawrence, KS freelance technical writer; Jill Glaser, University of Kansas Libraries Web Services Coordinator, and Joe Peterson, former University of Kansas Libraries Imaging Lab Assistant, for their attention to detail and willingness to proofread; to the Kenneth Spencer Research Library for the opportunity to work with its magnificent collections and to the Rare Books and Manuscripts Section Exhibition Awards Committee for its continued promotion of and support for library exhibitions, both physical and online.

Foreword

Institutions are eager to recruit online users to their digital collections. This can be seen in several trends: interest in joining online collaborative projects; increased administrative pressure to promote collections electronically to local and global communities; and expanded use of digital content in teaching and learning at all levels.

How an organization provides access to digital content is determined by the traditions of the institution, the creativity of the project manager, and the technical capacity of the organization. The staff resources available for such projects vary between institutions. They can range from an entire team—several content providers, web designers, programmers, exhibit designers and assistants—to a single staff member expected to quickly do it all.

Build It Once will help readers create a reliable, easily modified exhibition format that follows basic standards and best practices. It is designed for the staff member faced with the challenge of creating high-quality online exhibitions with limited exhibit experience, technical support and resources.

Increased opportunities and mandates to promote materials electronically bring new levels of sophistication to web development in small and large cultural institutions. Web technology advances have simplified the process of displaying images and text online for skilled web designers. However, for the community of willing, if reluctant, web designers who are without the benefit of training or savvy assistants, this book offers a straightforward set of procedures to aid in the creation of attractive, user-friendly exhibitions.

Liz Bishoff
University of Colorado at Boulder

Introduction

Every cultural institution, large or small, has something to shout about. Whether it is an eighteenth century diary found in a small county museum or a rich collection of beat poetry from a university library, hidden treasures reside on the shelves of our institutions and wait to be revealed. Online exhibitions are an effective tool to highlight and promote these unique materials. They enable users to navigate the archives of institutions worldwide and to access high-quality images and searchable text. Moreover, with curatorial assistance, these exhibitions can be turned into in-depth educational tools.

Because most libraries offer Internet access to their patrons, a vast amount of information is now accessible to users almost everywhere. We can only begin to imagine the benefits of this access for people in small and rural communities. Online access has become an invaluable outreach tool for libraries, museums, and archives hurrying to digitize collections and make them available to users online.

Build It Once is designed with untrained web authors in mind; those who find themselves confronted with the task of creating an online exhibition but who lack the confidence and skills necessary to begin the job. It is a book of practical practices designed to enable users to create web presentations that are straightforward, well designed and potentially award winning.

While online exhibitions vary in complexity, basic tenets apply to the design of fluid, descriptive, easily navigable displays. These principles are explained here, as is the basic structure for a flexible, easy-to-use exhibition format. Procedures are described for designing a simple format; for creating image and text files to populate the presentation; and for developing handcrafted web pages used to display each item with its descriptive text or metadata. An overview of available technologies that can simplify and shorten the task is also provided for those interested in increasing their skills.

Build It Once seeks to provide a focused and straightforward roadmap to exhibition creation and gives only a minimal look at the many important details of web authoring. Many books, manuals and websites exist—some of which are listed at the back of this book—that provide a wide range of in-depth instruction on the art of web design. Readers are encouraged to delve deeper into the specifics of web authoring if their interests or responsibilities in this field of study increase.

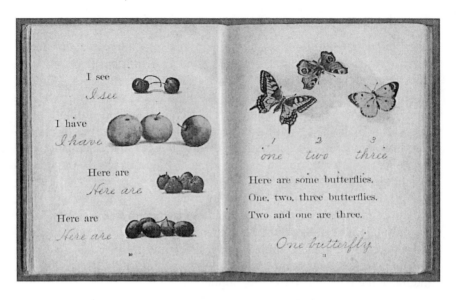

The Baldwin Primer, 1899

1

Define the Exhibition

Exhibition Impetus

Several trends feed the enthusiasm for online exhibitions. Participation in well-funded digital collaborations, the ongoing need to improve access to collections, and a growing fear that being without a digital presence will leave institutions behind and inaccessible are just a few of the motivators.

Partners in digital collaborations have not only been given the impetus to focus on a collection and increase its visibility, they will likely enjoy new funding for staffing or equipment and the benefit of institutional partners bringing new skills to the table. Administrative pressure to reach out to local and global communities from K-12 students to international scholars also fuels the demand for online representation. Web exhibitions help to meet this ongoing challenge and often bring the visibility necessary to garner new support from users.

Understanding the motivation behind the request for digital representation helps to define the audience and determine the necessary components of an online exhibition.

Audience

It may be difficult to identify the target audience of an online exhibition. Given the unlimited access to information on the World Wide Web, exhibitions may attract the interest of both expected and unexpected readers. The information displayed on your site needs to be understood by a wide audience of all ages. Avoid institutional jargon and undefined acronyms. Background material on the exhibition theme should be written with the casual visitor in mind and not assume previous knowledge on the topic. If, for example, primary resources are represented in a library exhibition, the descriptions of these resources must be understandable to users who are not rare book scholars.

Exhibition Size

The number of digital images included in your exhibition will determine how you proceed in building your web format. If a relatively small collection (one hundred or fewer items) has been selected for digitization, you will find that handcrafted pages representing individual images will serve you well. If, on the other hand, you will be working with a large number of items, this is the time to look into developing a database to manage the images and their metadata. You will most likely need to locate a database specialist who can design a database to manage multiple files or you can begin your own training in database design and dynamic web page development. This additional training could add eight to twelve months to your completion date. Determine the additional resources you will need if you decide database development is required and seek the approval from your administration to obtain necessary resources before proceeding.

Identify Resources

Once the exhibition has been defined and quantified and the audience has been considered, determine what resources currently exist for the project. Identify the people available to assist you so you can delegate and schedule digitization tasks. Consider equipment resources—both software and hardware. Do you have the tools necessary to perform the digitization tasks required? Until you know what your needs are, you won't be able to make this determination. See chapter two for information on equipment.

Design Considerations

Simplicity is your friend when designing an exhibition. Keep in mind that the main task is to present material in a clean, understandable way. Don't give in to pressure to make your design unduly complicated or overdone.

The Rare Books and Manuscripts Section (RBMS) Exhibition Awards Committee of the American Library Association (ALA) has added online exhibitions to its list of categories to receive the Katharine Kyes Leab & Daniel J. Leab American Book Prices Current Exhibition Award for printed exhibition catalogs and brochures. Evaluation criteria are documented by the committee to guide exhibition designers in creating award-winning presentations.

The design recommendations listed by the Awards Committee are simple and straightforward, calling for a well-considered, accessible design rather than a complex, highly technical one:

1. **Originality**. An electronic exhibition may adopt a background image or other feature appropriate to the topic of the exhibition.
2. **Appropriateness to subject matter**. While design elements need not directly reflect the subject matter of the exhibition, they should not confuse or compete with it.
3. **Effectiveness of design**. The design should work in practical terms as well as in aesthetic terms. Among the considerations are font, color, headlines, and graphics. Ease of navigation is of paramount importance.
4. **Typography**. Margins, font size, font style, and choice of colors are considerations. The typographical design and arrangement should not interfere with legibility.
5. **Multi-media and accessibility**. The exhibition should be accessible to as wide a user-base as possible. Additional multi-media features are encouraged, but applicants need to remember that not all necessary plug-ins will be in place in all browsers. If such elements are included, alternate pathways should be indicated. Your compliance with the American Disabilities Act, Section 508 will be viewed favorably by your audience.
6. **Quality of reproduction**. Size, register, focus, and sharpness are all considerations.

See appendix B for the complete list of criteria

2

Select the Equipment

If you are responsible for the imaging of exhibition materials, you will first need to review the selected materials and determine the format, size, and condition of each item. Such a review will allow you to determine the equipment you will need to safely and accurately digitize items. To simplify the inventory, divide items into the following categories:

- Two-dimensional—flat items such as photographs, manuscript pages, single leaves or unbound book pages.
- Slides, film, transparencies or negatives.
- Three-dimensional—oversized, unwieldy, or fragile items such as large maps, tightly bound books, brittle pages or museum objects.

When purchasing a scanner, talk to the sales representative about the following considerations that will influence the quality and the price of the scanner:

- Ease of use—some scanners are easier to use than others. Have the sales representative walk you through the scanning process.
- Scanning speed—the time it takes to scan each item will have a big impact on your digitization workflow. Let the sales representative know that you will be capturing images at a high resolution and need a scan speed estimate that reflects that.
- Bit depth—number of bits representing the color in one pixel. The greater the bit depth, the more colors displayed. Look for a scanner with a higher bit depth or dynamic range capacity.
- Resolution capacity—the number of pixels in a digital image. The higher the resolution, the greater the detail and quality. When evaluating a scanner's resolution, it is the 'optical' resolution that should be considered. The 'interpolated' resolution is a higher figure created by generating pixels with estimated values and inserting them into the image.

Hardware

Two-dimensional

Flat materials can, in most cases, be scanned using a flatbed scanner. An oversized flatbed scanner generally comes with a 12"x17" bed or glass. Large-format scanners are available but are expensive to buy and maintain and consume a fair amount of physical space. If your two-dimensional items are under 12"x17" and are not fragile or brittle, it's likely they can be scanned using a conventional oversized flatbed scanner.

- **Flatbed Scanner.** An oversized scanner can scan materials no larger than the dimensions of the bed, 11"x17."
- **Transparency Lid.** A special scanner lid that provides backlighting for scanning positive or negative film.
- **Automatic Document Feeder (ADF).** The ADF attaches to a flatbed scanner and allows you to automatically load multi-page documents into the scanner rather than scanning one page at a time.

Three-dimensional

Materials that cannot be placed on a flatbed scanner such as oversized, unwieldy, or fragile items, can be reproduced using an overhead scanner or a digital camera. These items can also be photographed with a conventional film camera. The film, slides or transparencies can later be scanned using a transparency lid on a flatbed scanner or, preferably for film or slides, by using a slide/film scanner.

- **Digital camera.** A high-end digital camera will allow for direct digital capture, unlike a traditional film camera. Correct lighting, however, is critical. A professional photographer may be needed to give recommendations on lighting and camera stands.
- **Copy stand.** The copy stand will hold the camera steady while providing a solid surface for the item being digitized.
- **Slide/film scanner**. If you plan to use a film camera to reproduce materials, a slide/film scanner is needed to then digitize the film. A separate attachment to the scanner that allows batch scanning can cut down on scanning time. Slide scanners are not

difficult to use but the additional step equals more time and money.

- **Overhead scanners.** Overhead scanners are very useful for scanning multi-page, bound items but often produce only black and white or greyscale images. Overhead scanners are still fairly expensive.
- **Scanning attachments or scanbacks.** Scanning attachments, used with medium and large format cameras, provide high-quality, high resolution color and black and white images but may be considered too slow for production scanning. These are very expensive pieces of equipment with a fairly steep learning curve.

Software

In addition to hardware, you will also have software needs in order to begin your project. These needs will be determined by the size and type of your exhibition, and specific software will be critical:

- **Web authoring software.** Web authoring software such as Mac-romedia Dreamweaver or Microsoft FrontPage takes your content and, based on what you tell it, arranges text, graphics, and images on each page of the online exhibition. HTML (Hypertext Markup Language) training is not a prerequisite for designing an online exhibition. However, a basic introduction provides a sense of familiarity that may reduce anxiety about learning this new skill and will assist you when working with the Web authoring software of your choice.
- **Imaging software.** Imaging software such as Adobe Photoshop allows you to manipulate the electronic images you have captured with your scanner or camera. You will use it to resize your image files, save them to different formats, create graphics and perform any other necessary image manipulation.
- **PDF (Portable Document Format) software.** Adobe Acrobat will be needed if you choose to create PDF files. PDF files are the most common technology for displaying text and graphics that can be printed exactly as they appear on screen. Printing directly from a web page is imprecise and may include unwanted elements such as the URL or date and time of printing. The Adobe Acrobat Reader is necessary for users wanting to read the

PDF files. This software is available free and can be easily downloaded from the Internet.

- **OCR (Optical Character Recognition) software.** OCR software such as Omni Page Pro will be necessary if text needs to be scanned as an image and then converted to a text format that can be searched and edited.
- **Application software.** All scanning hardware will be accompanied by driver and application software. A driver is used by your computer's operating system (such as Windows XP or Macintosh OS-X) to interact with a specific kind of hardware (such as a scanner or digital camera). Application software, on the other hand, provides a human user interface that allows you to issue commands to the hardware, save documents, and perform various kinds of modifications to documents.

The Evolving Imaging Lab

First Version

When we decided to create online versions of the exhibitions installed in the main gallery of the Kenneth Spencer Research Library at the University of Kansas, a few pieces of equipment were seen as critical to the process. These included, first and foremost, two computers with large amounts of RAM. We knew that we would be working with large images and various software packages so lots of RAM was important. We equipped these computers with large, high-quality monitors for accurate viewing of images and then purchased two oversized, 12"x17" flatbed scanners with transparency lids and automatic document feeders and a slide/film scanner with a batching attachment for scanning multiple scans.

A small digital camera was later donated to the lab and became our entry into digital photography. The camera was mounted to a 48" copy stand with two small lights that had been previously used by the library's photo archivist.

The library already owned an overhead digital copier. The overhead copier captured high-resolution images, in black and white only. The copier was used, primarily, to digitize text pages of bound books.

We were confident at that time that we had equipment that would easily serve our digitization needs, assist us in approaching accepted best practices for imaging, satisfy our conservation care and handling concerns, and allow us to develop a workflow that would ensure the ongoing creation of high-quality master images. This arrangement worked well while we were scanning flat, single-leaf objects. However, as more and more large or bound items came to the lab, it became clear that overhead scanning was the weak link in the imaging chain.

Our digital camera workstation was never intended for high-end photo lab work. The camera generated compressed files at a maximum dimension of 1500 x 1000 pixels and it lacked proper lighting. The resulting images were small, we were unable to save them in the uncompressed TIFF format, and the inadequate lighting distorted the image color. Consequently, no amount of post-capture image manipulation by the processor could really solve the problem.

Second Version

We decided that a higher quality camera was necessary for the studio work we would be doing. We purchased a 4.0 megapixel digital camera, an external flash and a battery recharger. The new camera was able to capture higher quality images in TIFF format. The external flash was a great improvement, particularly when we needed to take the camera out into the main gallery or other rooms of the library to capture items on-site.

The new digital camera increased the quality of our overhead imaging activities, but we were still some ways from producing publication quality images using a camera. Lighting continued to be a problem, even when using the camera's external flash. As with the smaller camera, accurate color continued to elude us. Each image had a blue or red cast that would take the processor some time to correct, if correcting was even possible. We were still relying on our original copystand and it was clear that the attached lights were not powerful enough to illuminate materials adequately. Another issue we were forced to confront was that the copystand allowed only 48 inches between the camera and the object photographed. This greatly limited our ability to shoot large items. Our humble alternative was to place oversized objects on a piece of black paper on the floor and hand-hold the camera while standing on a small ladder. Attempts to hold the camera steady while capturing images at the camera's highest—and slowest—setting prompted us to stop and rethink our arrangement once again.

Third Version

Two things happened at this point. First, a general collection review was undertaken to determine the percentage of materials that would need overhead digitization equipment in order to be reproduced. The collection review indicated that over 75% of items in the library's collections were candidates for overhead digitization. This information led to extensive research into high-end overhead scanning and photography equipment. The result of the research brought us to our current imaging lab configuration:

We continue to use our 12"x17" flatbed scanners and our slide/film scanner for film and the majority of two-dimensional materials. The overhead digital copier continues to be heavily used and has been upgraded to scan in grayscale rather than just black and white. The new grayscale setting allows the tones in a black and white photograph to be correctly represented. For color overhead copies, we now use a digital scanning attachment mounted on a 4x5 view camera. The camera itself is mounted to an 8 foot adjustable monostand and, although we started this arrangement with two 150 watt Buhl lamps on light stands, we have now upgraded to four lamps.

We have removed the fluorescent lighting from the ceiling in our studio space and painted the ceiling and walls black. We installed black carpeting and many large items are placed directly on the floor to be photographed. The carpet must be vacuumed regularly and extra care is always taken when photographing directly over collection objects.

It is clear that our current lab configuration will not remain static for long. Due to ever-changing technologies and advancements in digital photography, we assume that equipment and software will be upgraded on a fairly regular basis. However, we now have the capability to digitize materials by following a simple and streamlined workflow. We make an effort to capture our images at a consistently high level of quality and keep post-capture color manipulation to a minimum.

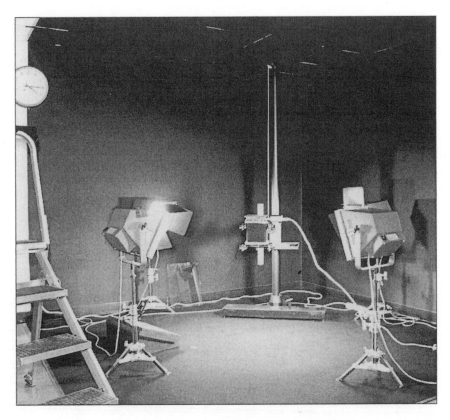

Figure 2.1: *KU Libraries Digital Imaging Lab*

3

Design the Format

Exhibition Format

When developing online exhibitions, create a simple hierarchy that divides the exhibition into manageable parts. Such a hierarchy simplifies development and allows the web designer to concentrate on the details that uniquely represent each collection. The basic organization of an online exhibition is in some ways similar to that of a book. The main page is not unlike the title page of a monograph. It leads the reader to the table of contents, the individual chapters, and the various subsections within each chapter.

Take time now to look at online exhibitions from other institutions. You will find that some of the best-looking presentations are not dependent on complicated animations or plug-ins but instead follow a simple and straightforward format, use effective navigational guides and rely on eye-catching graphics and images to capture users. Take note of the colors, graphics, text arrangement and display, logos and images. When you find a few sites that you like, imagine substituting your own material for what is currently being used. This will help you form a picture of your own exhibition and how it could look in the online environment.

Once you define and outline an exhibition, you will find that the individual levels of a hierarchy often present themselves automatically. Four levels are outlined here: the primary or home page followed by the second, third and fourth level pages. More complex exhibitions may require additional levels. See chapter eight, *Online Exhibition Tutorial*, for detailed instructions and cheat sheets on creating the following pages.

Home Page

The home page is the first and main page of an exhibition. It creates the reader's first impression and is the attention grabber for any online presentation. With just one screen, the home page tells users the name of the exhibition, the institution producing it, the theme being followed and the kind of material represented. The home page is the first, if not the main, opportunity to pique the interest of online visitors and convince them to enter and take time to browse. Provide readers with an overview of the exhibition and pertinent information about the exhibit sponsor at this first screen so they do not have to click deeper into the site to gain basic information.

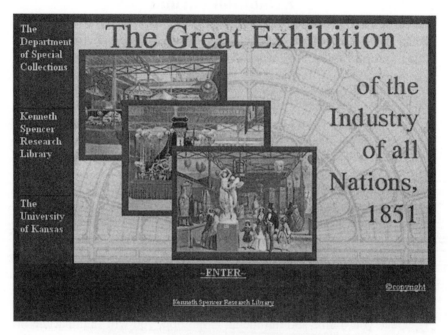

Figure 3.1: *Home page, "The Great Exhibition"*
University of Kansas Libraries

Second Level Pages

The second level pages in your exhibition are narrative pages. These pages are reached from the home page and provide textual information concerning such key areas as an introduction to the exhibition, descriptions of the different themes included, biographies of collection creators, and copyright text. The main content of the second level page will be narrative text describing each area of the exhibition; however, some components from the home page will be repeated on these pages, although less prominently, to assure that readers:

- consistently have the ability to move back and forth within the site
- always know the title of the exhibition they are visiting
- always know the name of the sponsoring institution

made buying trips.

"Family members and friends picked up on our enthusiasm for old textbooks, and we would occasionally receive a copy for a birthday or Christmas present, but nearly all the books were collected by ourselves.

"We gradually acquired some 1,800 books. They have been stored in every nook and cranny of our house. I sorted out the oldest and most delicate books, which we stored in their own bookcase in Jennifer's study. In our basement, we made a space to store the large number of textbooks written in the late 19th and early 20th century by women authors. Jennifer used this part of our collection as the basis for an article she did on women textbook writers for *Publishing Research Quarterly* and an entry on women textbook writers in *The Oxford Companion to Women's Writing in the United States* (1995).

"In keeping track of our collection, we noticed the large number of books published by Lindley Murray. This spurred my research, which culminated in the 1998 publication of *The Murrays of Murray Hill*, a study of the family and intellectual background of Lindley Murray. This book establishes that Lindley Murray was the largest-selling author in the world in the first four decades of the 19th century.

"About 40 of our primers were microfilmed by Professor Richard Venezky, of the University of Delaware, as part of his microfilm collection of American primers. Our collection also became the basis for *Writing the Past*, edited by Jennifer Monaghan and Arlene Barry, and published in conjunction with a historical display of literacy textbooks at the 1999 meeting of the International Reading Association in San Diego.

"We are donating our collection to the University of Kansas because of the presence there of an outstanding young scholar named Arlene Barry. We hope she will be able to make use of these textbooks as part of the reading education courses that she teaches."

return to content page

Kenneth Spencer Research Library · KU Libraries · University of Kansas · KSRL Exhibits

Figure 3.2: *History page, "Young American Readers"*
University of Kansas Libraries

Third Level Pages

The third level pages of the exhibition contain images and metadata. These pages may begin with narrative text concerning the selected themes and then list or display images and descriptive data for all exhibition items represented. Links to enlarged images or additional item-level description pages will be provided from the third level page if the exhibition requires it. Remember, allowing your readers to effectively navigate every page level is critical to successful exhibition creation.

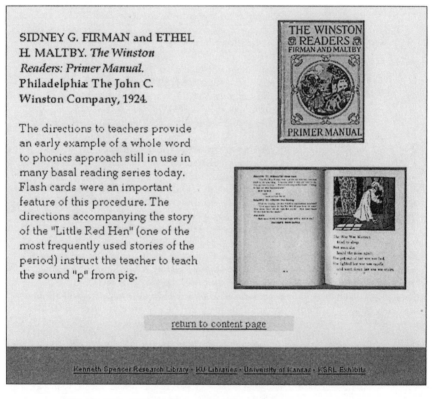

Figure 3.3: *Third level page, "Young American Readers"*
University of Kansas Libraries

Fourth Level Pages

The fourth level pages contain an enlarged version of images. Images should be inserted into HTML pages along with return buttons and navigation bars. Item-level metadata may also be found at this level, depending on the final design of the exhibition. Again, be sure your readers:

- consistently have the ability to move back and forth within the site
- always know the title of the exhibition they are visiting
- always know the name of the sponsoring institution

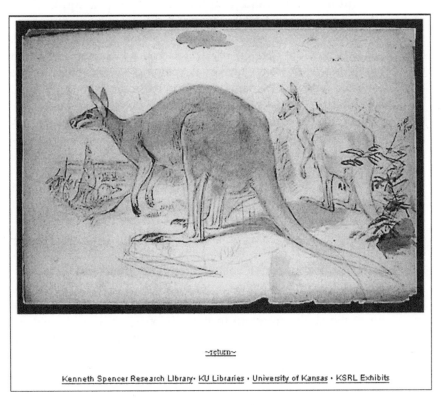

~return~

Kenneth Spencer Research Library· KU Libraries · University of Kansas · KSRL Exhibits

Figure 3.4: Fourth level page, "John Gould: His Birds and Beasts"
University of Kansas Libraries

Main Exhibition Components

Several basic components are necessary for each online exhibition you create. The following six components are usually displayed for the first time on the home page. Many will appear again on each additional page level. You may want to include others:

- **Exhibition title**. The title may be the same title given to a physical exhibition of the same material at your institution, or it may be an exhibition that was developed originally in electronic format. Either way, the title conveys the essence of the presentation.
- **Institution name (and graphic or logo, when applicable)**. Every page should include the name of your institution, but nowhere is it more important than on the home page, where users get their first impression of the material and of the institution providing access to it. Consider developing a presentation format for your institution's name that uses the same logo, color, and font. Insert it consistently at the same location on each page.
- **Representative images**. The first page need not display an image from the exhibition, but a key image or two that readily represent the selected material can go a long way in capturing the interest of your readers.
- **Navigation bar**. Often found at the top, bottom, or left side of each page, the navigation bar provides links to related sites that you want the user to be able to return to at any time while browsing the exhibition. Be sure to include a link to your institution – you never know what might spark a reader's interest and encourage him or her to search your site for more surprises.
- **Return button**. This allows your readers to return to either the home page or the table of contents at any time. Readers must be given the ability to return to the previous web page throughout the exhibition. Web authors cannot depend on the BACK button to achieve this. Give clear and easy access to the return button.
- **Copyright link**. This link is often found on the home page or on the table of contents page. Let readers know immediately what their responsibilities are when accessing an online exhibition and what your institution's intellectual property rights are.

4

Create the Structure

Web exhibitions are collections of web pages interacting with each other to represent books, manuscripts and images of all sorts. Using relative links, web authors are able to create virtual catalogs that enable readers to move from small thumbnail images to larger, richer, more detailed versions—as though walking through a gallery or reading room to take a closer look at an item of particular interest. By this time you've browsed the web and seen enough online exhibitions to have a basic idea of what captures your attention. With those sites in mind, get ready to create your own online display, custom-designed to highlight and accentuate those materials treasured by your own institution.

Web Content Accessibility

One of the first things to consider when creating your exhibition is accessibility to readers with disabilities. Making sure your web pages are accessible is not only a courtesy and a sound promotional step towards making your information available to the widest audience, it is mandated to federal agencies and increasingly expected from all web developers. A wealth of information is available on making websites that are accessible to people with disabilities. The World Wide Web Consortium (W3C) has published a list of Quick Tips (see appendix C). This list of key accessibility concepts will give you a head start towards making your online exhibition friendly to all users. Another suggestion, not included in the Quick Tips list, concerns colors used when creating hyperlinks on a web page. For those that cannot distinguish colors, colored links can prove troublesome. To test whether color contrast is sufficient to be read by people with color deficiencies, the W3C recommends you print your pages on a black and white printer (with backgrounds and colors appearing in grayscale) and check to be sure the links can be distinguished.

Style Sheets

Cascading style sheets (CSS) have become a standard way to format the text of a web document. They group formatting attributes (or styles) to define font color, size, alignment, link colors, etc throughout a site or exhibition. This structured formatting allows web pages to be displayed consistently across browsers. Style sheets not only simplify the HTML source code for web pages, they save designers a lot of time and effort if style changes need to be made (e.g., make all links blue instead of red) across an exhibition site. By using the same CSS for each web page within an exhibition, styles are implemented automatically. Web designers using CSS need only change the style sheet itself and each page within the site that includes the edited CSS file will be updated automatically.

If you have never used CSS, do not worry. Because they have been used to such great advantage in web design, style sheets are now considered a standard. Web authoring software makes it very easy for you to include them in your page design. Look in the Properties Inspector for CSS Styles. Select this and follow the instructions for setting the attributes you want. Save the style sheet and attach it to each of your exhibition pages as they are built.

Tables

When developing a web page, the table format can prove helpful by providing structure and consistency. The table gives you a border within which you can do your work. Once those lines have been drawn, you place your components inside and then move them around until you find the right fit.

Each web authoring software handles tables a little differently. Take time before you go any further to read though the table development instructions found in your program's user guide or reference manual. Here are the layout properties you must learn to use:

- **Table width**. You can set the table width using either a pixel dimension or a percentage of the browser window. Choose a percentage—this means that your table will take up the same portion of space on a user's screen, regardless of the monitor's size or resolution. Browser and operating systems handle tables in dissimilar ways and monitor size and resolution vary greatly among users. Because of this, it is important to opt for the greatest flexibility when setting the dimensions of your table. This is also important for accessibility.

- **Table alignment**. Tables are often preset to be aligned to the left side of the page. If you want your table in the center, or if you want it right-justified, be sure to reset its alignment.
- **Cell number**. The number of cells (columns and rows) will be based on how many components you need to place in your table.
- **Cell alignment**. Your table's columns and rows may require different alignment settings. For example, your navigation toolbar may be centered within the bottom row, but you may want your institutional name and logo left-justified at the top of the page. You can set each table cell individually.
- **Borders**. Borders can be visible or hidden. Their widths, colors, and textures can vary.
- **Background colors**. Select colors for any or all of the table cells.
- **Embedded tables**. Tables can be inserted into other tables. An embedded table allows more flexibility with content placement and the selective use of borders. Embedded tables must be used judiciously. If they are not nested in a clear order they become inaccessible to some users and difficult to edit. Such misuse of tables by web designers prompted the development of CSS as a page layout tool.

Tables will define the structure of each page level. The home page will have its own look as will the other pages. When you decide on the table layout that best serves the exhibition page you are working on, set the table properties and start moving your chosen components into the table cells.

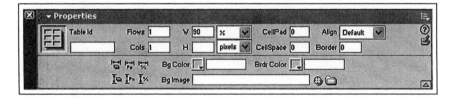

Figure 4.1: *Dreamweaver Table Properties Window*

Alternate Text Tags

Alternate text tags (alt tags) are HTML tags that provide textual information for non-textual elements such as images. In every web authoring software there is an option for attaching these tags to inserted images. The alt tag serves as a caption or title and displays each time the cursor is rolled over an image on a site. Alt tags should be attached to every image placed in the online exhibition. They are required for meeting Web Content Accessibility guidelines. They provide a written caption or title for images so that users who cannot or who prefer to not see images on a website know what item is being displayed. The title you have given to an image will display in a text box when the cursor moves over that image. This is a critical step in making your website accessible but it also is convenient and informative for anyone quickly browsing your pages.

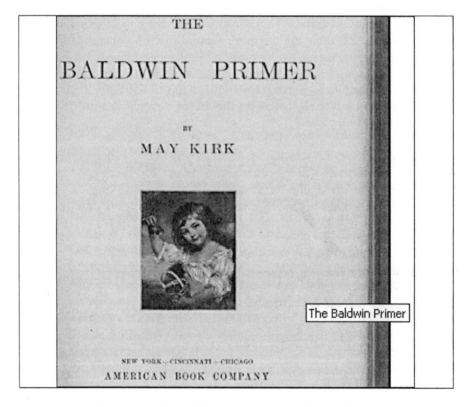

Figure 4.2: *"The Baldwin Primer," with displayed alt tag*

Links

In a basic sense, links provide the magic for any online display. They can take readers from a referring page to large, detailed images or rich additional information throughout the World Wide Web. Happily, creating links is a simple and straightforward process but it is helpful to understand the different types of links available. The two types covered in this book are relative links and absolute or external links. A relative link points users from one file within a site to another file in the same site. An absolute or external link will take users to locations outside the local site.

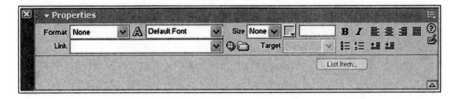

Figure 4.3: *Dreamweaver Link Properties Window*

5

Identify the Table Components

Create a Logo or Title Using Imaging Software

If you would like a stylistic title or logo for your exhibition, consider developing it using your imaging software. Special effects, elaborate fonts and images can be brought together to enhance the look of your site. In addition to giving you a more stylish look, headings or titles saved as images will be displayed consistently by any browser, alleviating fears of changing font styles or sizes and unpredictable spacing or layout.

Figure 5.1: *"Young American Readers" logo*

To create a graphic image like the one in Figure 5.1, follow these instructions:

- Open a new file in your imaging software.
- Insert an image.
- Select the TYPE or TEXT tool.
- Set the font style, size, color and special effects for your text.
- Type in the appropriate text.
- Move text body to the selected place in the image file.
- Crop the image and change the image size to necessary dimensions.

Save to a folder called "images"—as a GIF file if the image is text only or text and line art and as a JPEG file if the image includes a photo or full color art.

Build a Navigation Bar

Navigation bars provide links to related sites that you want your users to be able to return to at any time while browsing your exhibition. You should include the home page of your institution and you will probably want to provide access to the home pages of any project partners and perhaps the online catalog or search site of your institution. Once created, the navigation bar can be placed on each page of the exhibition.

KU Home | Libraries Home | Library Catalog | Kenneth Spencer Research Library

Figure 5.2: *Navigation Bar*

To create a navigation bar like the one above, follow these instructions:

- Open a new HTML page.
- Insert table, align to center of page, choose cell number and layout, colors and border size—your table will have one row and as many columns as you have navigation links.
- In each cell, type the name of an institution or department you want linked from the navigation bar.

- Highlight the name of each institution or department and create a link to its URL. If unsure how to create links, look at the entries for absolute and relative links in the manual or the online help link of your web authoring software.
- Save page as *navigation.htm* and put aside for later use.

Create a Copyright Page

Each online exhibition needs a copyright page. The copyright page contains a simple statement explaining the need for owner permission before using online material. It also gives a definition of your institution's intellectual rights and claims of ownership. It is a simple page to create and can save lots of time and difficulties if copyright infringement issues concerning exhibition materials ever surface.

Copyright Notice:

Original materials from which the digital images on this Web site have been derived may be protected by Copyright Law (Title 17 U.S. Code). You may use the digital images and information found on this Web site of the Kenneth Spencer Research Library for your private study, scholarship or research. If you wish to publish or reproduce the materials in any physical or digital form or use them for any commercial purpose, including display or Web page use, you must obtain prior written permission from the Department of Special Collections, Kenneth Spencer Research Library, University of Kansas Libraries. Please contact the Department of Special Collections by calling (785) 864-4334.

~return~

Figure 5.3: *Copyright Notice from "Young American Readers"*
University of Kansas Libraries

To create a copyright page like the one above, follow these instructions:

- Open a new HTML page.

- Insert a table. Your table will need to have at least two rows—one for the actual statement and one for a return box to take readers back to the exhibition.
- Type or cut and paste the text of the copyright statement you need to use for the exhibition.
- Insert an embedded table into your second row. The embedded table will have only one row and column and will contain text similar to that in the above table. Center your text and create a relative link to the homepage of your exhibition.
- Save the page as *copyright.htm*.

You can play with colors and borders but the development of this type of page will be simple and straightforward. The attached style sheet controls the font attributes. Be sure to attach the navigation bar.

Digitizing Images

Digitizing your materials is one of the first tasks you will undertake when creating an online exhibition. Be sure to give this job the time it needs; it is not a place for shortcuts. The quality of your scanning may determine the success of your exhibition.

Before you begin digitizing images, read through the following section and familiarize yourself with some of the vocabulary that is key to quality imaging. A basic understanding of file formats, compression, master and surrogate images, and filenaming will guide you as you create high quality images for your exhibition. Understanding these terms will enable you to capture and save your images according to accepted digitization standards and in so doing, ensure their accessibility to the many readers coming to your exhibition site.

Compression

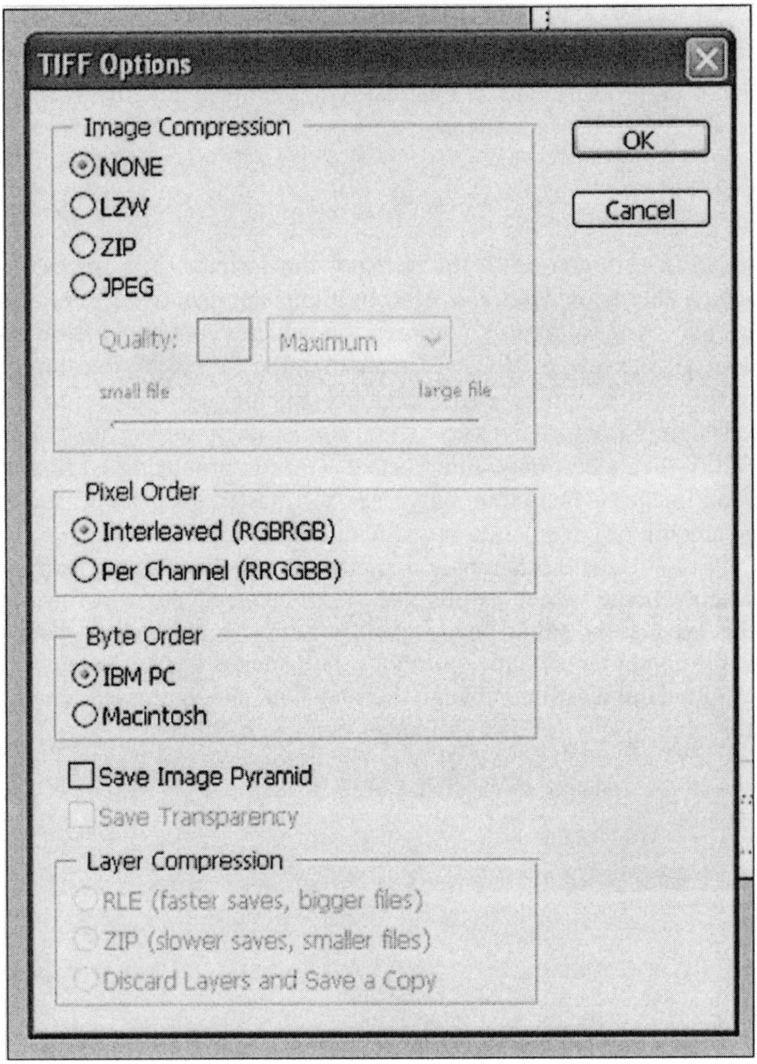

Figure 5.4: *Dreamweaver TIFF Lossless Compression Options*

Compression is a process through which image files are reduced in size. The *Collaborative Digitization Project (CDP) Glossary* defines compression like this: The reduction of image file size for processing, storage, and transmission. The quality of the image may be affected by the compression techniques used and the level of compression applied. De-compression is the process of retrieving compressed data and reassembling it so that it resembles its original form before compression (*See appendix C for the complete glossary*).

There are two types of compression, **lossless** compression which does not significantly affect the quality of the image and **lossy** compression which does degrade the image.

File Formats

Scanned images can be saved in many file formats. File formats allow images to be recognized and used by other applications. Some formats employ a lossy or lossless compression scheme enabling you to reduce the size of the image. You will recognize the format by the three-letter extension at the end of each filename (tif, jpg, gif). Three commonly used standard file formats are:

TIFF—Tagged-image File Format—format producing large, uncompressed images. Most commonly used for master images because of the large amount of information saved with each image.

JPEG—Joint Photographic Experts Group—employs a lossy compression scheme, which results in a significant reduction in file size but at the expense of some image quality. JPEG is the format most often used for photographic and continuous tone images displayed online.

GIF—Graphics Interchange Format—an uncompressed image format used primarily for line art images displayed online.

Figure 5.5: *Photoshop file format drop-down list*

Master images

Follow the industry goal of "scanning once." This means creating a high quality scan of each item. The scanned file is then used, rather than the original, whenever requests are made to reproduce the item. Save your masters in the TIFF format using, if any, LZW lossless compression (you will be given this compression choice when you save the file in your photo editing software). The quality of the scan is dependent on the resolution and bit depth settings chosen at the time of capture. Because high quality image capture results in large file sizes, adequate storage space is required. Storage space is not freely available and can be a critical issue for many institutions. Keep in mind, however, that if you store and maintain your master images carefully, the scans you produce now will serve your institution far into the future.

Surrogate images

Once the master scans have been captured and saved in the TIFF format, you will need to create smaller copies, or surrogates, of each image for display on the web. Typically, a small image (thumbnail) of each item is created to allow users to quickly see the different materials in the collection. A larger version (reference) is then created with a higher resolution and larger dimensions so the user can get a good look at the details of the individual image. Some exhibitions offer two reference versions in order to provide even more detail to viewers. If you plan to offer large reference versions on your site, include a note containing the file size and an explanation to users that larger files take longer to open. Full color and photographic surrogate images should all be saved in the JPEG format. Line drawings can be saved in the GIF format.

Sample Surrogate Image Dimensions:

- Thumbnail—150-200 pixels on long dimension at 72 ppi.
- Referencefile 1—500-600 pixels on long dimension at 72-90 ppi.
- Reference file 2—800 pixels on long dimension at 72-150 ppi.

File Sizes

The size of a digital image is measured in bytes:
kilobytes (KB) = 1,000 bytes
megabytes (MB) = 1,000,000 bytes
gigabytes (GB) = 1,000,000,000 bytes
File size is proportional to the pixel dimensions of an image; images with more pixels will have a larger file size. Large image files will produce more detail but require more disk space to store and are slower to print and load.

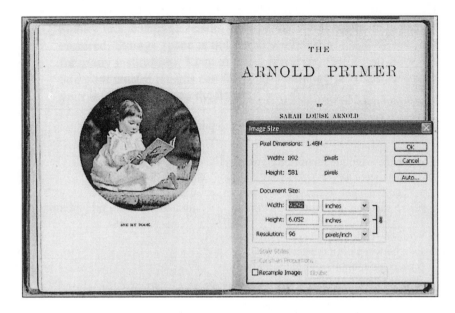

Figure 5.6: *Photoshop's Image Size Screen*

Imaging Considerations

Exhibition scanning is time consuming because it involves many steps. Scan as close to master quality as you can and save these images in the TIFF format *(see File Formats above for definitions of image formats)*.

This will result in a large, high quality, uncompressed image that can later be used to create any lower-resolution or surrogate copies you need for this or future projects. Master scans (scanned between 300-600 ppi, depending on the item) will result in large files ranging anywhere from 5–50 MB per file (or larger). If you are short on storage, solve this problem first. The images will need a safe, maintainable home. This means uploading your files to an institutional server or burning them to CD-ROM or DVD.

Filenaming and Structure

Every image file you create will need a unique identifier or filename. Institutions use different filenaming conventions when managing images.

Here is a basic configuration that is followed by many involved in image management programs:

Description	Example
institutional acronym	ksrl, unct, csla
departmental acronym (when applicable)	pd, kc, sc, gi
object ID—unique identifier given to original, such as: ▪ *call number or accession number* ▪ *a succinct descriptive identifier -*	▪ c1250, a6730, 899cd76 ▪ linnaiportrait or goreyinterior
version—code letters used to differentiate between digital versions (i.e., master, thumbnail, reference) of the original item	m, s, t, r
file extension—three letter extensions which represent the file format	tif, jpg, gif

Figure 5.7: *Filenaming Convention*

Here are two examples of filenames that follow this structure:

- *ksrl.sc.c1250_t.jpg*
- *unct.kc.goreyinterior1_r.tif*

File Storage

Save image files to an image folder within your collection folder so that all are easily located and managed. For example:

When all your surrogates are created and stored in a file directory such as the one shown above, you can browse, select and insert them into the HTML pages of your exhibit. Have your images accurately sized before you insert them. Resizing an image after it has been placed on the page can skew the proportions of the image. In addition, if the image is large, but resized to be smaller on the page, the file size is not reduced and can take a long time to appear.

6

Build the Web Pages

Home Page

Figure 6.1: *Home page table from "Young American Readers"*
University of Kansas Libraries

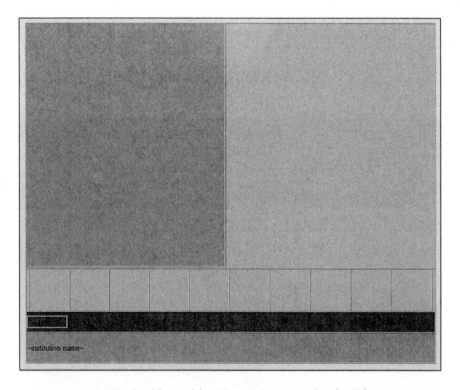

Figure 6.2: *Blank table used for "Young American Readers" home page shown in figure 6.1*

Chapter three identifies the basic components of the home page: exhibition title, institution name, representative image(s), copyright link and navigation bar. Once all these components have been determined, begin inserting them or typing them into their appointed cells. To insert an image, click on the table cell that will hold the image and follow the editor's instructions for inserting images. You'll be given the opportunity to browse back to the image folder within your exhibition site and from there you can select the image you need. Remember, have your images accurately sized before you insert them into the table. Make sure images are aligned properly and choose the font, size, and color for any headings that have not been saved as images (*see chapter five—Table Components*).

In figure 6.1, the table is divided into three rows:

- The top row has been divided into two columns. The exhibition title has been typed into the right cell and a single-cell table has been embedded into the cell on the left. An image from the exhibition has been inserted into the embedded table and a border has been given to the same table.
- A table has been embedded into the second row. This table has one row and ten columns. It too has been given a border and images have been inserted into each column.
- The single-cell embedded table in the third row is just large enough to hold the link taking users to the secondary page. It has been given a different background color than the underlying table and so stands out.

As you add content to your table, you may have second thoughts about the layout or design of your page. If you decide, for instance, that the layout should be redesigned, the background colors lack contrast or that you need fewer or more images, don't worry—changes can easily be made at this point. Split and merge your cells until you find a preferred layout and cut and paste your content to repopulate the table. There are many ways to structure one's home page. Examples of different sites are shown below. Each example appears unique, yet all follow the same basic table structure. By varying background colors, border preferences, cell layout, etc designers are able to give sites a different look and feel. The same will be true for the exhibitions you will soon be creating. They may all share a recognizable design or each may stand-alone with its unique presence.

Figure 6.3: *Home page, "John Gould: His Birds and Beasts"*
University of Kansas Libraries

Figure 6.4: *Home page, "Langston Hughes: A Voice for all People"*
University of Kansas Libraries

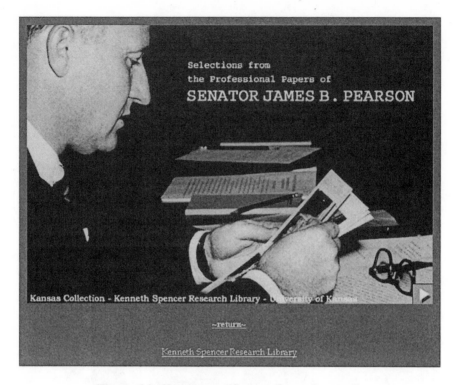

Figure 6.5: *Home page, "Senator James Pearson"*
University of Kansas Libraries

Second Level Pages

Second level pages are generally narrative pages. They are linked from the home page and provide descriptive information about the exhibition and its creators. Because you may have several pages at this level, each potentially populated with very different content, be prepared to lay out the table for each page differently. Second level pages will need a return button to take readers back to the home page. Place the button in the bottom row of the table.

The steps you followed to create the home page apply to the second level pages as well:

- Open and give a title to a new HTML page.
- Attach style sheet.
- Insert table, align to center of page, choose cell number and layout, colors and border size.
- Insert embedded tables, if necessary.
- Insert images.
- Type in necessary text.
- Link to all appropriate third level pages.
- Create a return box which returns to the home page.
- Attach navigation bar.

Examples of other page types include a content page and a conservation page. Each page will suggest its own table structure:

Content page

A content page is a complex page similar to a table of contents. A page like this will list the different themes or formats that make up the exhibition itself. It will likely contain images—one or several—as well as the exhibition title, the institutional logo, a return button and the navigation bar.

The content page will also include links to the third or item-level pages of your exhibition. You can design the content page in many ways. Each exhibition and its individual structure will drive the design of this page. Let the content determine how the table is developed.

Figure 6.6: *Content page, "Young American Readers"*
University of Kansas Libraries

Conservation page

Creating a conservation page gives you an opportunity to promote the conservation efforts of your institution. If you have any items that need to be repaired before they can be hung in a gallery exhibit or digitized for an online exhibit, document the work as it is done and place images and descriptive text on one of your second level pages.

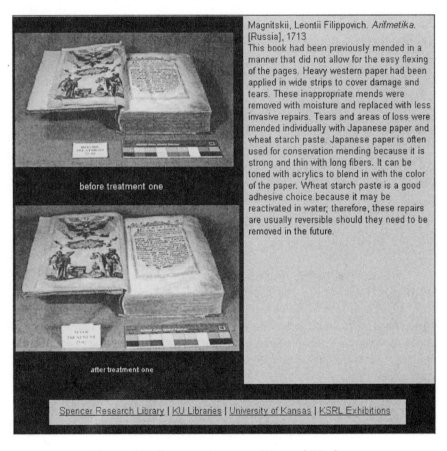

Figure 6.7: *Conservation page, "Frosted Windows: 300 Years of St.Petersburg" University of Kansas Libraries*

Third Level Pages

The third level pages contain the item-level descriptions of exhibition materials. It deserves repeating that if your exhibition contains a large number of items, investigate developing a database to manage your images and metadata. If, however, you are dealing with a manageable number, the following procedure for creating handcrafted web pages should serve you well and enable you to display your exhibition materials simply and clearly.

As with the home page and the second level pages, a table is used to define the layout of the pages at the third level:

- Open and give a title to a new HTML page.
- Attach style sheet.
- Insert table, align to center of page, choose cell number and layout, colors and border size.
- Insert embedded tables, if necessary.
- Insert images.
- Type (or cut and paste) in necessary text.
- Create links to appropriate fourth level pages such as enlarged image versions.
- Provide return buttons to the appropriate second level pages.
- Insert navigation bar.

These pages make up the nucleus of your exhibition. Their design should be kept simple and focus on the images and associated text. Below find examples of third level pages that demonstrate some of the different layout possibilities. The table inserted into a third level page can hold the images and metadata, any additional narrative text, and a return button. The number of images in the division determines the structure of this table.

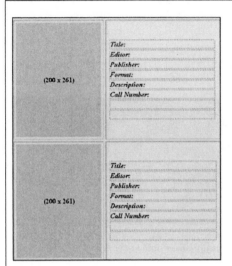

Figure 6.8: *Sample table listing images and metadata vertically*

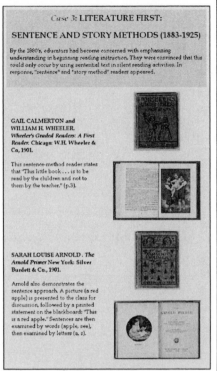

Figure 6.9: *Vertical, scrolling item-level list, "Young American Readers" University of Kansas Libraries*

One way to deal with a small number of images is to use a two-column table with enough rows to hold all the images and metadata for that page. Users can scroll down and see each image displayed.

Another way to address the layout of a third level page is by using a multi-columned table with as many rows as is necessary.

(176 x 65)	(176 x 65)		(176 x 65)	(176 x 65)
Title:	*Title:*		*Title:*	*Title:*
Date:	*Date:*		*Date:*	*Date:*
Publisher:	*Publisher:*		*Publisher:*	*Publisher:*
Description	*Description:*		*Description*	*Description:*
(176 x 65)	(176 x 65)		(176 x 65)	(176 x 65)
Title:	*Title:*		*Title:*	*Title:*
Date:	*Date:*		*Date:*	*Date:*
Publisher:	*Publisher:*		*Publisher:*	*Publisher:*
Description	*Description:*		*Description*	*Description:*

Figure 6.10: *Sample table listing images and metadata horizontally*

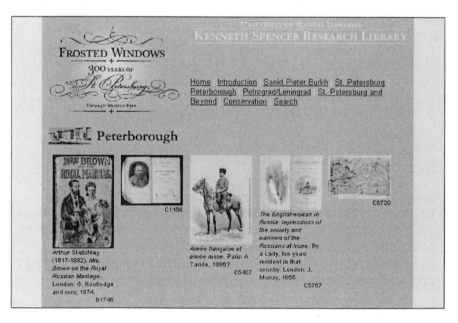

Figure 6.11: *Horizontal display of materials,*
"Frosted Windows: 300 Years of St. Petersburg"
University of Kansas Libraries

Create Multiple Pages

It is likely that each level of the exhibition hierarchy will require more than one page to represent the selected material and themes or formats. Templates can be created using your web authoring software to lock in the design of a page so it can be used over and over again with new content each time. You can forgo template building, however, by building just one page per level. Before you add any content to the table structure, save the page and use it as a template for any additional pages. Copy it as many times as you need to in order to have pages for each level of your exhibition. Save each copy with its own filename, title and correct return link.

Use your "template" to create a third level page, empty of content, for each division of your exhibition. You can populate the pages with thumbnail images and associated metadata. Each page will need a return button to take readers back to the secondary page from which it was linked.

Fourth Level Pages

Fourth level pages contain enlarged image versions of exhibition materials. Readers viewing image thumbnails on the third level pages can click on an image (or the item title, depending on the page design) and move to another HTML page that displays a large reference version of the image. The fourth level pages may include descriptive information about the item but will certainly include a return button allowing the reader to go back to the third level page they just left.

As with the home page and the second and third level pages, a table is used to define the layout of the pages at the fourth level:

- Open and give a title to a new HTML page.
- Attach style sheet.
- Insert table.
- Insert images.
- Type (or cut and paste) any necessary text.
- Provide return button with relative link to the appropriate third level page.
- Insert navigation bar.

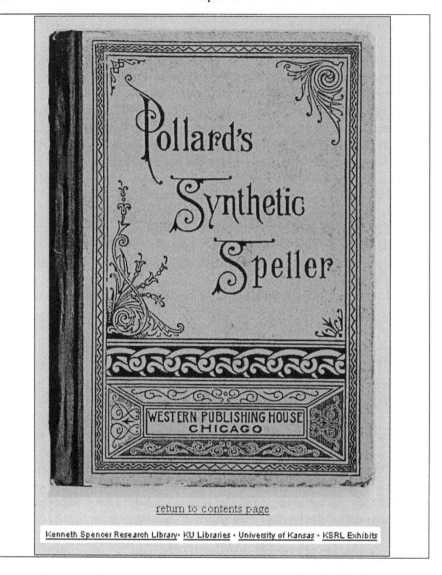

Figure 6.12: *Image enlargement page, "Young American Readers"*
University of Kansas Libraries

7

Advanced Topics

Increased opportunities and mandates to promote materials electronically have brought new levels of sophistication to web development in small and large cultural institutions. Web technology advances have simplified the process of displaying images and text online for skilled web designers, however, maintaining an advanced skill set and keeping up with technological innovations can be a full time job. Below find a quick definition of a few of the many tools available to web designers in their efforts to create efficient and effective web products.

1. **CSS as Page Layout Tool**. CSS layout uses style sheets to define the precise placement of elements on a web page. Layout information is determined through an external cascading style sheet file that allows designers to make changes in one place rather than modifying each page. CSS as a page layout tool is particularly useful when several pages share the same design or structure.

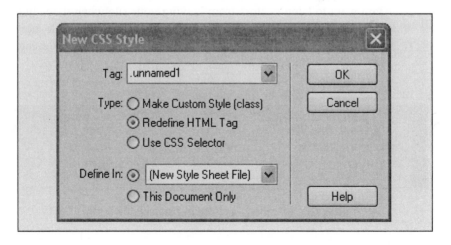

Figure 7.1*: Dreamweaver CSS Style Window*

2. **Layers.** Experienced web designers like using layers for page layout because they allow a greater level of control and versatility than tables. Like tables, a layer serves as a container for HTML content. But in the case of layers, they can be positioned exactly where you want them on the page and can be overlapped or hidden by additional layers. Web authoring software makes layers easy to work with. You need only draw a layer on the page where you want an image or text to appear and then insert an image or other element in the layer. If you need to reposition the layer, you can drag it to a new position in the document.

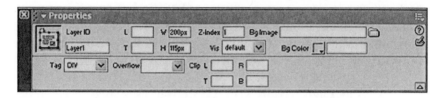

Figure 7.2: *Dreamweaver Layers Properties Window*

3. **Frames.** A page with frames looks like a single web page but each link on the page targets a unique document within its own frame or window. If you want a main part of your page, such as the main toolbar, to always be visible when the page is open or if you want to keep visitors from leaving your site when they click on external links, consider using frames when linking to new content. However, pages with frames can be difficult to create and problematic to view.

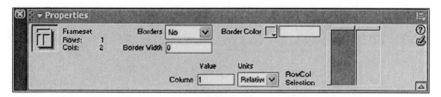

Figure 7.3: *Dreamweaver Frames Properties Window*

4. **Templates**. Templates can help you create web pages with a consistent design and layout. They make it easy to update and maintain pages. Templates lock in the design of a page so it can be used over and over again with new content each time. The template feature in web authoring software enables you to designate areas of a page that can be changed while everything else on the page remains fixed. This feature can be helpful if you're turning production work over to someone else and want to assure that some basic elements are unaltered.

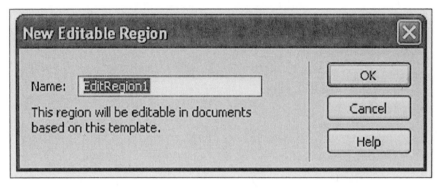

Figure 7.4: Dreamweaver Template Editable Region Window

8

Online Exhibition Tutorial
Macromedia Dreamweaver MX

Figure 8.1: *Good Reading Primer*

1. Introduction to Dreamweaver
2. Where to Begin
3. Dreamweaver Tools
   a. Document Window
   b. Toolbars—Document and Standard
   c. Property Inspector
   d. Library
   e. Tag Selector
   f. Preview in a Web Browser
4. Set up a local site
5. Create and save a new page
6. Create and attach style sheet
7. Creating relative and absolute links
8. Create tables

9. Create and insert navigation bar
10. Insert images
11. Insert or create text
12. Step by Step Instructions

Introduction to Dreamweaver

This short tutorial provides step by step instructions for creating online exhibition web pages using Macromedia's Dreamweaver web authoring software. This tutorial was created using Dreamweaver MX. As you probably know, Dreamweaver is not the only web authoring software available nor is there just one version of Dreamweaver that users have access to. For those users who have not selected software to build their web exhibition, or if your institution provides access to Dreamweaver and you have yet to become familiar with it, the following tutorial will assist you to build a straightforward and efficient online exhibition that you and your institution can be proud of. If you are using a different version than Dreamweaver MX, consult the manual or help screens if and when you are confronted with software inconsistencies. In addition, know that this tutorial gives just a small snapshot into Dreamweaver. There are many more tools, activities, procedures and shortcuts than are described here. See the *Bibliography* in the back of this book for two suggested Dreamweaver manuals that can greatly assist in using this powerful software.

Where to Begin

In basic terms, an online exhibition is a managed group of web pages representing a chosen theme or format. Pages are organized into folders that reside in a site, or master location. You will have two copies of your site, one that sits on your own computer and a mirror copy that sits on a remote server and provides access to the web.

Before you go any further, determine where the site will reside on both the local disk and the remote server. Will your institution provide server space? Or will you have to obtain this remote access from some other means? Once these questions have been answered and your remote site has been established, launch Dreamweaver and begin to familiarize yourself with the look and feel of the display.

Dreamweaver Tools

There are many tools in Dreamweaver to assist in building web pages.

This tutorial will emphasize a few of these but users are encouraged to take time to explore the many additional menus and windows offered by the software. Any initial familiarity will assist you as you proceed.

- **Document Window**
  The main window on the Dreamweaver screen is the Document Window. It holds the current document you are working on. The Title Bar across the top of the window displays the page title and the filename. An asterisk displayed beside the filename indicates that the file is unsaved. The Document Window allows three views of your page: the Design View, the Code View and a split screen titled the Design and Code View. The Design view allows you to view your page approximately, though not exactly, as it will appear in a web browser. The Code View is the actual HTML source code. It is helpful to take a look at the HTML code so you can get an idea of the tags and how they work. The split screen divides the Document Window into two parts so you can see the Design and Code Views together.

- **Toolbars—Document and Standard**
  There are two toolbars in addition to the main menu that open by default when you launch Dreamweaver. If they don't open automatically, you will have to open them manually.

  - To open the Document toolbar:
    Choose View>Toolbars>Document—The Document toolbar lets you name or re-name your pages; switch between the Design and Code Views; preview in the browser and refresh your pages.

  - To open the Standard toolbar:
    Choose View>Toolbars>Standard—The Standard toolbar allows you to open a new page; open an existing file; save your files; cut, copy and paste, undo/re-do.

- **Property Inspector**
  The Property Inspector is a panel that opens at the bottom of your page and allows you to edit different page elements. Available properties appear in this panel when an element is selected. These properties automatically change depending on the page element selected. It is convenient to keep this window

open all the time but if you ever find it closed, reopen it by choosing Window>Properties.

- **Library**
  Dreamweaver's Library stores the original HTML code for frequently used elements such as images, bodies of text, and tables. These elements are called Library Items and can be copied or borrowed from the Library each time you want to add them to a web page. Examples of Library Items could be navigation bars attached to every page, copyright notices or contact information included in every online exhibition. A great advantage to the Library is that items can be created and attached to web pages but if changes to the item are later necessary, only the item itself need be edited. All web pages containing the item are upgraded automatically.

- **Tag Selector**
  The Tag Selector is very useful for selecting elements on the web page that need to be edited. Using the cursor to drag across an element to highlight it can be unreliable in Dreamweaver because it is sometimes difficult to select the actual element you want. Selecting the HTML tag displayed in the bottom left corner of the Document Window will highlight the element you want to edit quickly and accurately.

- **Preview in a Web Browser**
  Dreamweaver allows you to preview the page you are developing through the web browser of your choice. You will have a good idea of the look of your page as you work in the Document window but the browser preview allows you to see your page as it will be displayed online. Click the F12 key or go to File>Preview in Browser> Edit Browser List to choose the primary and secondary browsers you will be using. Because browsers display websites differently, it is best to preview your site in more than one browser. Not only will this preview help you to develop your site, it will give you the satisfaction of seeing your work as the public will see it. Use the preview tool freely and often.

Set up a local site

The first thing to do as you prepare to develop an online exhibition or website in Dreamweaver is create a local site. The local site, or master/main folder, is the storage location on your own computer for all the files that make up your website. The relative links in your HTML pages point to pages stored in various sub-folders in the local site. Setting up the local site correctly ensures that these links are created accurately.

You will eventually create both a local and a remote site. These two sites are mirror images of each other. The local site holds the working, under development versions of each page until they are ready to be published online. At that point they are transferred to the remote site and accessible to the public.

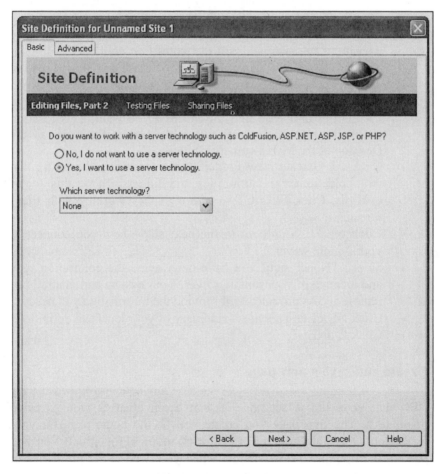

Figure 8.2: Dreamweaver Site Definition Window

- Open Dreamweaver.
- Choose Site>New Site.
- Choose the Basic tab—you will then be asked to enter a name for your site.
- In the text box, enter a name to identify the site. Name the site **my_sites**.
- Click NEXT to proceed to the next step.
- Click NO when asked if you want to work with a server technology (you can change this if you later advance to working with a database and creating dynamic pages).
- Click NEXT to proceed to the next step—how you want to work with your files.
- Select: "Edit local copies on my machine, then upload to server when ready (recommended)." The simplest and most forgiving way for beginners to develop an online exhibition, or any website, is to create and edit the pages first on the local disk, or hard drive, and then upload copies of those pages to a remote web server where they are then available on the world wide web.
- Click the folder icon next to the text box and browse down the list of files until you find the location you want. This location should be one you can find quickly and easily, such as the Desktop or the My Documents folder.
- Click the "Create New Folder" button to create the folder that will hold your exhibition files and folders. Name this folder **exhibits**. Click SELECT to return to the "working with files" screen.
- Click NEXT to proceed to the next step—how you connect to your remote server.
- Select: "None" until you have determined the connection type and location of your remote server. Your system administrator or remote access provider will provide the information you need.
- Click NEXT and receive a summary of your local site definition.
- Click DONE.

Create and save a new page

Now that your site is set up, you can begin creating web pages to populate it. The first page you create will be the home page for your exhibition. Open the Property Inspector (Window>Properties). You will rely on the options in this window when you need to set properties or attributes to your elements in your documents. When you started

Dreamweaver, a blank HTML document was automatically created. Close that document and create a new page.

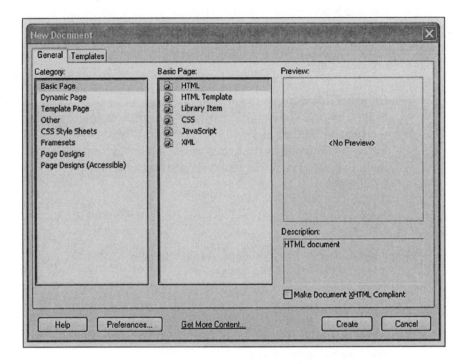

Figure 8.3: *Dreamweaver New Document Window*

- Choose File>New.
  In the Category box select Basic Page. The middle column will now be relabeled Basic Page—choose HTML.
- Click Create. A new page appears.
- In the title text box of the Document Toolbar enter the title of the page. Make the title descriptive and complete, such as, "*Monaghan History of Reading Collection.*" This title is located within the <head> tag in the HTML code of your document. Search engines on the Web will index this title so you want it to accurately describe the document. In addition to a title, you are also able to add keywords and a description to the <head> tag of your document. It is recommended that you do this so that different search engines will index your site so users can locate it.

- Choose Insert>Head Tag>Keywords to add keywords to the
  <head> tag. Type in multiple keywords representing your document and divide them with commas.
- Choose Insert>Head Tag>Description to add a document description to the <head> tag.

Save Your New Page

- Choose File > Save As.
- In the Save As dialog box, browse to the **exhibits** folder inside
  the site root folder.
- Enter the filename **index.htm** (the default name for the first or
  main page of each folder in a website is *index.htm*).
- Click Save.

Create CSS style sheet

- Choose Text > CSS Styles > New CSS Style.
- Type—select "Redefine HTML."
- Define in—select "New Style Sheet File."
- Tag—from the drop down list of all available CSS tags select
  "body." The body tag represents the text body of the document.
- After selecting "body" click OK. The "Save Style Sheet File"
  window has now opened.
- Select "File System" as the location to select your file name.
- "Save In" text box—browse to the **exhibits** folder within the
  my_sites root folder.
- Click the Create New Folder button to create a folder for your
  style sheets. Name this folder **styles**.
- File name text box—enter the name **basic**.
- Click OK. The "CSS Style Definition" for the window "body"
  tag has now opened.
- Select "type" in the Category box.
- Font—from the drop down list select the font you want to use for
  the body, or text, of your entire exhibition.
- Color—if you want your text to be something other than the
  default black, select the color here.
- If there are any other options from the "CSS Style Definition"
  box that you want to apply to text body of your site, select them
  now.
- Click OK.

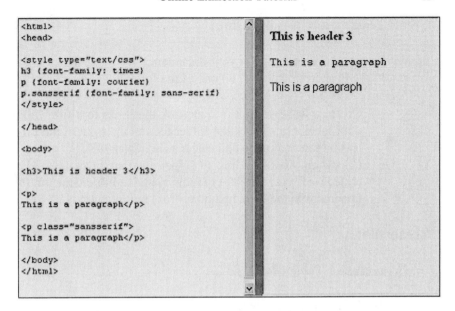

Figure 8.4: Dreamweaver CSS Style Window

If there are any other tags you want to define for the entire exhibitions site, i.e., background color, repeat this same procedure for each tag. If you want the various links in your site to display in colors other than the default blue for links and purple for visited links, you can define them by selecting "Use CSS Selector" instead of selecting "Redefine HTML" in the Define in: drop down list. Choose the different types of links from the Tag: drop down list (one at a time) and follow this same procedure.

Attach Style Sheet

- Choose Text > CSS Styles.
- Define in—select "Attach Style Sheet" from drop down list.
- File/URL text box—browse to **my_sites/exhibits/styles.**
- Select **basic.css.**

Your **basic.css** style sheet is now attached to your home page, **index.htm**. You will attach this same style sheet to every page you create in your exhibition. If at some point you decide to change any of the display settings you have defined through the style sheet you need only edit and save the **basic.css** settings and all your pages will be updated.

Create relative and absolute links

- Select text or an image in your document.
- In the Property Inspector, do one of the following:

    - Create a Relative link (a hyperlink that links to a file within your local site)—click the folder icon to the right of the Link text box to browse to and select a file. Click OK.
    - Create an Absolute link (a hyperlink that links to a page outside of your site)—type the path and filename of the document in the Link text box. Press return/enter.

Create tables

Dreamweaver Table Glossary:

Table Id—ID for the table.
Rows and Cols—number of rows and columns in the table.
W and H—width and height of the table in pixels, or as a percentage of the browser window's width *(the height of a table is more accurately determined by the dimensions of the inserted content and is best to leave blank here).*
CellPad—number of pixels between a cell's content and the cell boundaries.
CellSpace—number of pixels between adjacent table cells.
To be sure that browsers display the table with no padding or spacing, set Cell Padding and Cell Spacing to 0.
Align—determines where the table appears, relative to other elements in the same paragraph such as text or images. Left aligns the table to the left of other elements (so that text in the same paragraph wraps around the table to the right); Right aligns the table to the right of other elements (with text wrapping around it to the left); and Center centers the table (with text appearing above and/or below the table). Default indicates that the browser should use its default *(left)* alignment.
Border—specifies the width, in pixels, of the table's borders. To be sure that browsers display the table with no border, set Border to 0. To view cell and table boundaries, give border a number value.
Clear Column Widths and *Clear Row Heights*—delete all

explicitly specified row height or column width values from the table.

Convert Table Widths to Pixels and *Convert Table Heights to Pixels*—buttons set the width or height of each column in the table to its current width in pixels (also sets the width of the whole table to its current width in pixels).

Convert Table Widths to Percent and *Convert Table Heights to Percent*—buttons set the width or height of each column in the table to its current width expressed as a percentage of the Document window's width (also sets the width of the whole table to its current width as a percentage of the Document window's width).

Bg Color—table's background color *(white)*.

Brdr Color—color for the table's borders.

Bg Image—table's background image.

Create table

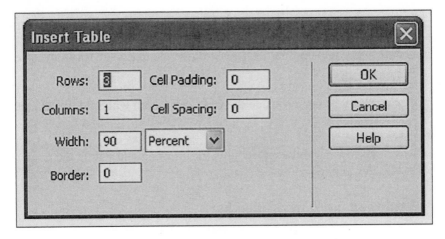

Figure 8.5*: Dreamweaver Insert Table Window*

- Insert>Table.
- Set the table properties you have determined in the "Insert Table" box on your screen. When setting the width of your table, choose "percentage" from the drop down list. By setting the table width based on a percentage of the screen's width, you can be assured that the table will display consistently on different monitor screens.
- Click OK—a table appears on the page.

- Select the complete table. Forget how to select elements in the Document Window? See *Tag Selector* on page 3.
- In the Property inspector, set, or reset, additional table properties. This is only necessary if you want properties other than the default: *See the table glossary above for an explanation of each property.*

   - Align—from the drop down list select where on the screen you want to position the table.
   - Border—enter a number to represent the thickness of the border (1 being finest) or 0 if you do not want a border.
   - Bdr and BG color—select colors for the border and background.
   - Horz and Vert—from these drop down lists set the text alignment for each table cell.

Embed a table

There may be times when you will have the need for a separate, or embedded, table within an existing table. Embedded tables have an independent set of table properties and can give the designer flexibility when laying out a page.

- Place the cursor inside the table cell which will hold the embedded table.
- Insert>Table.
- Follow the above procedures for inserting and setting the properties of a table.

Create and insert navigation bar

- Insert>Table.
- Select 1 row and the number of columns needed to represent the addresses in your navigation bar.
- Select border size (if any) and color of table background (if any)
- Select the alignment of your navigation bar from the align text. box in the Property Inspector—this will determine where on the page the navigation bar will reside.
- Select all cells in your navigation bar and then choose the text alignment for your cells from the Horz/Vert text boxes.
- Type a destination name into each cell of the navigation bar.

- To turn a destination name into a relative link (a hyperlink that links to a file within your local site)—highlight the destination name, click the folder icon to the right of the Link text box and browse to the selected file.
- To turn a destination name into an external link (a hyperlink that links to a page outside of your site)—type the path and filename of the document in the Link text box.
- Select the completed navigation bar.
- Choose Modify>Library>Add object to library.
- Choose Window>Assets.
- In the "Assets" panel under the "Library" category, a new item will appear called "Untitled." Rename this file **navbar**.
- You have now created a navigation bar and can drag it from the Library in the Assets panel onto the document you are working on.

Insert images

- Put your cursor inside a table cell that will hold an image.
- Choose Insert>Image.
- In the "Select Image Source" window browse to: images/exhibits/my site. All the images you have created should be found in this folder—correctly sized and divided into folders by image format. Browse to the correct image and click on the filename. A single click will display a thumbnail of the image with dimensions and file size. *If you select an image in a folder outside of the root folder, Dreamweaver will ask you if the image can be copied to the root folder. Say "yes" and browse to the images folder and save the image there.*
- Click OK to insert image.
- Select inserted image.
- In the Property inspector:
  - Border—enter a number to display a border around the image.
  - Alt—enter a short title or description for the image or graphic.
  - Link—browse to and select the appropriate relative link or enter an external link.
  - Align icons—to control the alignment of an image within a body of text, select the chosen position here.
  - V and H Space—used to create a margin of space around the image to keep text from creeping too close to the image. En-

ter the number of pixels of space—vertically and horizontally—you want around the image.

- Repeat this process for all images inserted onto the page.

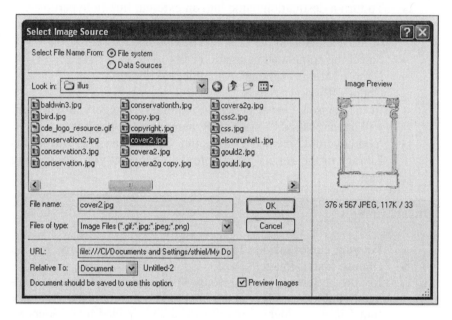

Figure 8.6: *Dreamweaver Select Image Source Window*

Insert text

- Enter new text or select existing text from a word document or another HTML page.
- Choose Edit>Copy.
- Place your cursor in the selected table cell.
- Choose Edit>Paste.
- Edit your table cell properties and your text as necessary.

Step by Step Instructions

Home Page Cheat Sheet

Create new page:

1. Choose File>New
2. Select Basic Page > HTML
3. Click Create
4. Title—enter page title
5. Choose Insert>Head Tag>Keywords. Type in multiple keywords divided by commas.
6. Choose Insert>Head Tag>Description. Type in a document description.
7. Choose File>Save As
8. Enter filename **index.htm**
9. Click Save

Add Style Sheet:

1. Choose Text>CSS Styles
2. Type—select "Attach Style Sheet"
3. Browse—**my_sites/exhibits/style/basic.css**
4. Click OK

Insert navigation bar:

1. Choose Window>Assets>Library (open book icon)
2. Highlight **navbar**
3. Click "Insert" at bottom of Assets panel—navigation bar will appear in document window
4. Place cursor above Navigation Bar in document window

Insert table:

1. Choose Insert>Table
2. Rows—enter "4"
3. Columns—enter "1"
4. CellPad and Space—enter "0"
5. Width—enter "85" "percent"
6. Border—enter "0"

7. Click OK

Specify table properties:

1. Open Properties Inspector
2. Align—select "center"
3. Place cursor in top row of table
4. Click "Split Cells" button
5. Split Cell Into "Columns"
6. Number of Columns—enter "2"
7. Place cursor in second row
8. Choose Insert>Table
9. Rows—enter "1"
10. Columns—enter "5"
11. CellPad and Space—enter "0"
12. Width—enter "85" "percent"
13. Border—enter "1"
14. Click OK
15. Place cursor in third row

Embed table:

1. Choose Insert>Table
2. Rows—enter "1"
3. Columns—enter "1"
4. CellPad and Space—enter "0"
5. Width—enter "10" "percent"
6. Border—enter "0"
7. Align—left
8. Click OK

Insert text:

1. Place cursor inside table
2. Horz—select "center
3. Vert—select "middle
4. Type the word "enter"
5. Place cursor inside fourth row
6. Align—right
7. Type the word "copyright"
8. Merge and Split cells as needed to house all necessary components in home page

9. Place cursor in table cells and insert images, graphics or text
10. Create relative links to secondary pages ("enter" and "copyright")
11. Choose File>Save As
12. Select—**index.htm**

Congratulations—you've just completed your home page!

Step by Step Instructions

Second Level Page Cheat Sheet

Create new page:

1. Choose File>New
2. Select Basic Page>HTML
3. Click Create
4. Title—enter page title
5. Choose Insert>Head Tag>Keywords. Type in multiple keywords divided by commas.
6. Choose Insert>Head Tag>Description. Type in a document description.
7. Choose File>Save As
8. Enter filename, i.e., **copyright.htm**
9. Click Save

Add Style Sheet:

1. Choose Text>CSS Styles
2. Type—select "Attach Style Sheet"
3. Browse—**my_sites/exhibits/style/basic.css**
4. Click OK

Insert navigation bar:

1. Choose Window>Assets>Library (open book icon)
2. Highlight **navbar**
3. Click "Insert" at bottom of Assets panel—navigation bar will appear in document window

4. Place cursor above navigation bar in document window

Insert table:

1. Choose Insert>Table
2. Rows—enter "2"
3. Columns—enter "1"
4. Cell Pad and Space—enter "0"
5. Width—enter "85" "percent"
6. Border—enter "0"
7. Click OK
8. Open Properties Inspector
9. Align—select "center"
10. Place cursor in first row of table
11. Type or cut and paste the text of the copyright statement
12. Place cursor in second row

Embed table:

1. Choose Insert>Table
2. Rows—enter "1"
3. Columns—enter "1"
4. CellPad and Space:—enter "0"
5. Width—enter "10" "percent"
6. Border—enter "0"
7. Click OK

Create return link:

1. Place cursor inside table
2. Horz—select "center"
3. Vert—select "middle"
4. Type the word "return"
5. Highlight "return"
6. Link—browse to **my_sites/exhibits/index.htm.** You have now created a relative link to the home page
7. Save As—**copyright.htm**

Congratulations—you've just completed a second level page!

It is likely that you will need more than one second level page for your exhibition. The page you have created can now be used as a template. To create a new second level page simply select and copy the original page; open new page and paste text into it. Be sure to change the information in the head tags; correct the address in the *return* link; add appropriate text and images; and save the new page with a unique filename.

Step by Step Instructions

Third Level Page Cheat Sheet

Create new page:

1. Choose File>New
2. Select Basic Page > HTML
3. Click Create
4. Title—enter page title
5. Choose Insert>Head Tag>Keywords. Type in multiple keywords divided by commas.
6. Choose Insert>Head Tag>Description. Type in a document description.
7. Choose File>Save As
8. Enter filename **div1.htm**
9. Click Save

Add Style Sheet:

1. Choose Text>CSS Styles
2. Type—select "Attach Style Sheet"
3. Browse—**my_sites/exhibits/style/basic.css**
4. Click OK

Insert navigation bar:

1. Assets>Library (open book icon)
2. Highlight **navbar**

3. Click "Insert" at bottom of Assets panel—navigation bar will appear in document window
4. Place cursor above navigation bar in document window

Insert table:

1. Choose Insert>Table
2. Highlight table
3. Rows—enter "2"
4. Columns—enter "2"
5. Cell Pad and Space—enter "0"
6. Width—enter "85" "percent"
7. Border—enter "1"
8. Align—center
9. Place cursor in the top right table cell
10. Align icon—select the center icon

Embed table:

1. Choose Insert>Table
2. Rows—enter "6"
3. Columns—enter "1"
4. CellPad and Space—enter "0"
5. Width—enter "30" "percent"
6. Border—enter "0"

Insert text:

1. Highlight all table cells
2. Horz—select "left"
3. Vert—select "middle"
4. Place cursor in first table cell
5. Enter "Title:"
6. Place cursor in first table cell
7. Enter "Author:"
8. Place cursor in first table cell
9. Enter "Date:"
10. Place cursor in first table cell
11. Enter "Format:"
12. Place cursor in first table cell
13. Enter "Description:"
14. Place cursor in first table cell

15. Enter "Call Number:"
16. Highlight table
17. Edit>Copy
18. Place cursor in the bottom right table cell of the original table
19. Edit>Paste

Insert images:

1. Highlight all tables in first or left column
2. Horz—select "left"
3. Vert—select "middle"
4. Place cursor in top left table cell
5. Insert>Image
6. Browse—**my_sites/exhibits/images/jpgs_th** and double click on the appropriate thumbnail image.
7. Highlight image
8. Border—1
9. Alt—enter a short title or description for the image or graphic
10. Repeat steps 57 through 61 to insert additional images
11. Use cursor to select and drag table cell borders to adequately wrap images and metadata
12. Save As—**div1.htm**

To add additional rows to the original table, highlight the table and change the number in the **Rows: box**. Continue inserting images in the left column table cells and embedding tables in the right column cells.

Congratulations—you've just completed a third level page!

It is likely you will need more than one third level page for your exhibition. The page you have created can now be used as a template. To create a new third level page simply select and copy the original page; open new page and paste text into it. Be sure to change the information in the head tags; correct the address in the *return* link; add appropriate text and images; and save the new page with a unique filename.

Step by Step Instructions

Fourth Level Page Cheat Sheet

Create new page:

1. Choose File>New
2. Select Basic Page > HTML
3. Click Create
4. Title—enter page title
5. Choose Insert>Head Tag>Keywords. Type in multiple keywords divided by commas.
6. Choose Insert>Head Tag>Description. Type in a document description.
7. Choose File>Save As
8. The filename for each fourth level page is the same as the image filename. The htm extension will identify the file as an HTML page, i.e., **ksrl.scmon23.htm**
9. Click the Create New Folder button to create a folder for your fourth level pages. Name this folder **pages**.
10. Within the **pages** folder, create a new folder for each Division in your exhibition
11. Name these folders **Div1, Div2, Div3.**

Add Style Sheet:

1. Choose Text>CSS Styles
2. Type—select "Attach Style Sheet"
3. Browse—**my_sites/exhibits/style/basic.css**
4. Click OK

Insert navigation bar:

1. Choose Window>Assets>Library (open book icon)
2. Highlight **navbar**
3. Click "Insert" at bottom of Assets panel—navigation bar will appear in document window
4. Place cursor above navigation bar in document window

Insert table:

1. Choose Insert>Table
2. Rows—enter "2"
3. Columns—enter "1"
4. Cell Pad and Space:—enter "0"
5. Width—enter "85" "percent"
6. Border—enter "0"
7. Click OK
8. Open Properties Inspector
9. Align—select "center"
10. Place cursor in first row of table
11. Horz—select "center"
12. Vert—select "middle"
13. Place cursor in second row of table

Embed table:

1. Choose Insert>Table
2. Rows and Columns—enter "1"
3. Cell Pad and Space—enter "0"
4. Width—enter "10" "percent"
5. Border—enter "0"
6. Click OK

Create return link:

1. Place cursor inside table
2. Horz—select "center"
3. Vert—select "middle"
4. Type the word "return"
5. Highlight "return"
6. Link—browse to the appropriate third level page. You have now created a relative link back to the thumbnail image.

Insert images:

1. Insert>Image
2. Browse—**my_sites/exhibits/images/jpgs_r** and double click on the appropriate reference image
3. Highlight image

4.   Border—1
5.   Alt—enter a short title or description for the image or graphic
6.   Repeat steps 44 through 48 to insert additional images
7.   Save each page to the appropriate Division folder in the pages
     folder:
     my_sites/exhibits/pages/div1/ ksrl.scmon23.htm

Congratulations—you've just completed a fourth level page!

You will have many fourth level pages. The page you have created can
now be used as a template. To create a new fourth level page simply select and copy the original page; open new page and paste text into it. Be
sure to change the title and the information in the head tags; correct the
address in the *return* link; add appropriate text and images; and save the
new page with a unique filename.

Conclusion

At this point you have created four page layouts: the home page and second, third and fourth level pages. These pages will make up the structure of your online exhibition and can be copied and reused for any future exhibition that may come your way. As stated earlier, the step-by-step instructions give only a small snapshot into Dreamweaver web authoring software. There are many more tools, activities, procedures and shortcuts than are described here and it is likely that you will want to learn more. Read the Dreamweaver manual; there are also many helpful tools available online. Don't be daunted by the task of creating an attractive, useful online exhibition. Experiment with different ideas. Try a variety of fonts, background colors, borders and layouts. The look and style of your exhibition will be defined by the materials chosen for display. Look at each item carefully, note the colors and patterns, the period represented, the mood—allow yourself to have fun, be creative and remember to *save* often. If you change your mind, you can always *undo* and go back to where you started.

Remember, you are building a fluid, descriptive and easily navigable exhibition structure. Your informative text, quality images and descriptive data; your accurate return buttons and navigation bars will all fit easily into this structure. The end result will be an effective, well-considered online exhibition.

Figure 8.7: Work That is Play, 1920

Appendix A

Rare Books and Manuscripts Section

Association of College and Research Libraries

A Division of the American Library Association

Leab Exhibition Awards Evaluation Criteria

The following criteria are used by the RBMS Exhibition Awards Committee in evaluating entries for the Katharine Kyes Leab & Daniel J. Leab *American Book Prices Current* Exhibition Awards for printed exhibition catalogs and brochures. No point scale is provided since individual judges may assign a different weighting to each factor.

- Catalogs
- Brochures
- Electronic Exhibitions
- Submission Guidelines and Entry Forms

Electronic Exhibitions

Electronic Exhibitions are produced for distribution on the World Wide Web or on other digital media. They serve as gateways to library or archival materials. An electronic exhibition need not be based on a physical exhibition but it must describe the materials from a distinct point of view.

- **Intellectual Content**
1. Originality
2. Overall informational content
3. Accuracy of detail and bibliographical description
4. Apparatus
5. Organization and presentation
6. Choice of items

7. Illustrations
8. Appropriateness to intended audience
9. Contribution to scholarship
- **Design**
1. Originality
2. Appropriateness to subject matter
3. Effectiveness of design
4. Typography
5. Multi-media and accessibility
6. Quality of reproduction

Explanation of Electronic Exhibition Evaluation Criteria

Electronic Exhibition Intellectual Content 1. Originality of content.
The subject matter of the electronic exhibition is original, or is treated in a highly original way.

Electronic Exhibition Intellectual Content 2. Overall informational content. There should be a sense that the subject is covered adequately for the aims of the exhibition. These aims can be determined partly by looking at Intellectual criterion 8, Appropriateness to intended audience, and Design criterion 2, Appropriateness to subject matter. For someone totally new to the exhibition's subject, one question to ask as a basis for judgment is, "What did I learn from this exhibition?" Another is, "What would a typical (or the specified) audience for this exhibition learn from it?" Many exhibitions do not purport to be definitive treatments of the subject matter. Still, each exhibition must offer enough information to satisfy a viewer's desire for basic knowledge.

Electronic Exhibition Intellectual Content 3. Accuracy of detail and bibliographical description. Facts, grammar, spelling, and syntax should be correct. Bibliographical description may range from simple author, title, and publication data all the way to accounts of binding, provenance, media, and illustration processes, physical structure, etc., as appropriate. The sources of images should be properly cited.

Electronic Exhibition Intellectual Content 4. Apparatus. This includes at the very least, the title and dates (if applicable) of the exhibition, the name of the host institution, and information about the electronic exhibition's author, date of creation, and designer. There should be a complete table of contents or site map for exhibitions. There may also be acknowledgments, a preface, a bibliography, and links to related resources.

Electronic Exhibition Intellectual Content 5. Organization and presentation. This refers to the content, not the layout of the electronic exhibition. Does the information flow in a natural or logical manner and is the writing clear and understandable?

Electronic Exhibition Intellectual Content 6. Choice of items. The range of objects featured must convey a thorough sense of the topic.

Electronic Exhibition Intellectual Content 7. Illustrations. Clearly, the use of graphics in an electronic exhibition differs from that in a printed catalog. More graphics can be featured in exhibitions than in printed catalogs, but graphics should still be germane to the exhibition and enhance understanding of the topic. If all items cannot be illustrated, the most significant or visually arresting should be chosen for reproduction.

Electronic Exhibition Intellectual Content 8. Appropriateness to intended audience. The entry form requires identification of the intended audience. The exhibition text should neither be over the heads nor too rudimentary for the intended audience. Considerations are the level of writing and the extent and depth of coverage of the topic.

Electronic Exhibition Intellectual Content 9. Contribution to scholarship. An electronic exhibition may fill in an area where there is little scholarship or may become a reference tool or basic text in its field. It may take a new and valuable approach to an old and overworked topic. In the absence of subject expertise, judges will also look at the depth of coverage and information provided in the exhibition about its relationship to existing scholarship in the field.

Electronic Exhibition Design 1. Originality of design. An electronic exhibition may adopt a background image or other feature appropriate to the topic of the exhibition.

Electronic Exhibition Design 2. Appropriateness of design. While design elements need not directly reflect the subject matter of the exhibition, they should not be antithetical to it.

Electronic Exhibition Design 3. Effectiveness of design. The design should work in practical terms as well as in aesthetic terms. Among the considerations are font, color, headlines, and graphics. Ease of navigation is of paramount importance. See *Suggested Practices* at the end of the design criteria.

Electronic Exhibition Design 4. Typography. Margins, font size, font style, and choice of colors are considerations. The typographical design and arrangement should not interfere with legibility.

Electronic Exhibition Design 5. Multi-media and accessibility. The exhibition should be accessible to as wide a user-base as possible. Additional multi-media features are encouraged, but applicants need to remember that not all necessary plug-ins will be in place in all browsers. If such elements are included, alternate pathways should be indicated. Compliance with American Disabilities Act, Section 508 will be viewed favorably.

Electronic Exhibition Design 6. Quality of reproduction. Size, register, focus, and sharpness are all considerations.

Suggested Practices for the Design of Electronic Exhibitions:

- Have content outline (toc) available on every page, either as a full toc or a 1-click link to the full toc.
- If "splash screens" are used, be sure to include a "SKIP INTRO" link.
- If a site incorporates pop-up windows, have them close automatically or launch them into the same second browser window or include clear CLOSE buttons, so users are not left with many open windows across the bottom.
- Consistency in design is also important for the effectiveness of design. For example, the placement of navigation (and all) buttons should remain the same throughout all the pages.
- Try to avoid long scrolls and if long scrolls are necessary, have a printer-friendly version.

Leab Exhibition Awards Evaluation Criteria. 2003. Rare Books and Manuscripts Section, American Library Association. http://www.rbms.nd.edu/committees/exhibition_awards/

Appendix B

collaborative
digitization
program

Digitization Glossary

Archival Image
An image meant to have lasting utility. Archival images are usually kept off-line on a cheaper storage medium such as CD-ROM or magnetic tape, in a secure environment. Archival images are of a higher resolution and quality than the digital image delivered to the user on-screen. The file format most often associated with archival images is TIFF, or Tagged Image File Format, as compared to on-screen viewing file formats, which are usually JPEGs and GIFs.

Archival Scans
Digital images serve as surrogates of the original. At this point in time, there is no such thing as an Archival or Preservation scan that acts as an exact replica or replacement of the original, as it is not yet possible to record every piece of information found in the original with today's scanner technology.

Artifacts
Visual digital effects introduced into an image during scanning that do not correspond to the original image being scanned. Artifacts might include pixellation, dotted or straight lines, regularly repeated patterns, moire, etc.

CCD Array
Charge-Coupled Device array. Light sensitive diodes used in scanners and digital cameras that sweep across an image during capture and, when exposed to light, generate a series of digital signals that are converted into pixel values.

Compression/Decompression
The reduction of image file size for processing, storage, and transmission. The quality of the image may be affected by the compression techniques used and the level of compression applied. Decompression is the

process of retrieving compressed data and reassembling it so that it resembles its original form before compression. There are two types of compression:

Lossless compression is a process that reduces the storage space needed for an image file without loss of data. If an image has undergone lossless compression, it will be identical to the image before it was compressed. Primarily used with bitonal images.

Lossy compression is another process that reduces the storage space needed for an image file, but it discards information (information that is "redundant" and not perceptible to the human eye). If an image that has undergone lossy compression is decompressed, it will differ from the image before it was compressed, even though the difference may be difficult for the human eye to detect.

There are both standard and non-standard compression techniques available. In general, it is better to employ a compression technique that is supported by standards, non-proprietary, and maintained over time. In selecting a compression technique, it is necessary to consider the attributes of the original. Some compression techniques are designed to compress text, others are designed to compress pictures.

Derived Image (Derivative Image)

An image that has been created from another image through some kind of automated process, usually involving a loss of information. Techniques used to create derived images include sampling to a lower resolution, using lossy compression techniques, or altering an image using image processing techniques.

Digital Camera

Copystand scanners that resemble microfilming stands. The digital camera directly captures an image without the use of film. Source material is placed on the stand and the camera is moved up or down in order to fit the material into its field of view, which allows for the scanning of a range of differently-sized materials. Resolution of digital cameras is usually fixed and is expressed as a pixel ratio.

Digital Image

An electronic photograph scanned from an original document, made up of a set of picture elements ("pixels"). Each pixel is assigned a tonal value (black, white, a shade of gray, or color) and is represented digitally in binary code (zeros and ones). The term "image" does not imply solely visual materials as source material; rather, a digital image is simply a representation of whatever is being scanned, whether it be manuscripts, text, photographs, maps, drawings, blueprints, halftones, musical scores, 3-D objects, etc.

Digital Library
Definitions of the digital library range from narrow to broad, with some disagreement on the actual function of a digital library. Clifford Lynch defines the digital library as "an electronic information access system that offers the user a coherent view of an organized, selected, and managed body of information." This definition recognizes the more traditional role of a library in the digital world: at the very least, a digital library should offer services along with information, such as indexing or cataloging. Users of digital library resources may come to expect (and already do expect) more sophisticated functions, such as information and knowledge management services, resource discovery mechanisms, and personalization of access and monitoring of new and existing digital resources. In his paper, "What is a Digital Library? Definition, Content and Issues," Harter discusses the properties of a digital library in terms of several categories on a scale from the narrow view to the broad. Some of the concepts he considers include: types of information resources: selection, organization, and authority control of information resources; authorship; physical and logical location of resources; access to resources; who are the defined user groups; and what services are offered and by whom (or what)? The Task Force on Archiving Digital Information makes a further distinction between digital libraries and digital archives. The Task Force defines digital archives as "repositories of digital information that are collectively responsible for ensuring, through exercising various migration strategies, the integrity and long-term accessibility of the nation's social, economic, cultural, and intellectual heritage instantiated in digital form." Digital libraries, on the other hand, collect and provide access to digital information, but they may or may not provide long-term storage and access to that information.
The Association of Research Libraries also has a good definition of a digital library.

Diodes
Light-sensitive electronic components used by the scanner during image capture. Diodes sense the presence or absence of light and create a digital signal that the computer then converts into pixel values.

Dots per inch (dpi)
A measurement of the scanning resolution of an image or the quality of an output device. DPI expresses the number of dots a printer can print per inch, or that a monitor can display, both horizontally and vertically.

DTD
Document Type Definition. Documents are regarded as having types, just as other objects processed by computers do. The type of a document

is defined by its constituent parts and structure. A DTD defines the structure of an SGML (Standard Generalized Markup Language) document.

Dublin Core

(Definition taken from http://www.purl.org/dc). A metadata element set intended to facilitate discovery of electronic resources. Two features of the Dublin Core metadata element set are simplicity and extensibility. Dublin Core is intended to be usable by both non-catalogers and specialists alike, to provide an economic alternative to more elaborate descriptive models such as full MARC cataloging, and be flexible enough to encode the structure and semantics inherent in rich descriptive standards. The Dublin Core seeks to promote a commonly understood set of descriptors to help facilitate interoperability across disciplines. The Dublin Core can be mapped to the MARC record and a variety of output structures can be generated.

Dynamic Range (Bit-depth)

The number of colors or shades of grey that can be represented by a pixel. The smallest unit of data stored in a computer is called a bit. Dynamic range is a measurement of the number of bits used to represent each pixel in a digital image. **1-bit or bitonal** means that a pixel can either be black or white. Bitonal imaging is good for black and white images, such as line drawings and text. However, scanning in grayscale rather than bitonal may produce a better looking image. **8-bit color** or **8-bit grayscale** means that each pixel can be one of 256 shades of color or one of 256 shades of gray. **24-bit color** means that each pixel can be one of 16.8 million colors.

EAD

Encoded Archival Description. The EAD is an SGML (Standard Generalized Markup Language) DTD (Document Type Definition) intended to assist in the creation of electronic finding aids. Developed at UC-Berkeley, it is now maintained and supported as a standard by the Library of Congress and sponsored by the Society of American Archivists. The EAD can be used to represent complete archival structures, including hierarchies and associations. The kinds of functionality that EAD affords can also be implemented using Dublin Core, and it is also possible to migrate records from Dublin Core into the EAD format if necessary. More information on EAD is available at http://www.loc.gov/ead

File Size

The file size of an image is proportional to its resolution. The higher the resolution, the bigger the file size. File size is different from image size.

Flatbed Scanner
An image capture device much like a photocopier. The object to be scanned is placed face-down on a glass plate. The CCD array passes beneath the glass.

GIF
Graphic Image File Format. A widely supported image storage format promoted by Compuserve for use on the web.

Gray Scale
A range of shades of gray in an image. Gray scales of scanners are determined by the number of grays, or values between black and white, that they can recognize and reproduce.

HTML
Hypertext Markup Language. An encoding format for linking and identifying electronic documents and used to deliver information on the World Wide Web. May be superceded by XML in the future.

Image Capture
Using a scanner or other device to create a digital representation or electronic photograph of an image. The scanning process is often labor-intensive and costly, requiring a substantial investment in handling and processing original materials and their surrogate images. The current strategy is to capture an image at the highest resolution appropriate to the original, and store it off-line as an archival image on CD-ROM or magnetic tape. Techniques such as lossy compression and subsampling can then be used to create derivative images for use online. In the future, as the ability to deliver high-quality archival scans develops, it will be possible to place the archival scan online without cost of recapture. Scanning can be done in-house or contracted out to a vendor. Whether scanning is done in-house or outsourced, quality of the images can vary widely. Image specifications should be stated clearly in the contract with the vendor and sample images (at varying resolutions) of the materials to be scanned should be requested of the vendor prior to the start of the project.

Image Manipulation or Alteration
Making changes (such as tonal adjustments, cropping, moire reduction, etc.) to an image using image processing software.

Image size
Describes the actual physical dimensions of an image, not the size it appears on a given display device.

JPEG
Joint Photographic Experts Group. A compression algorithm for condensing the size of image files. JPEGs are helpful in allowing access to full screen image files on-line because they require less storage and are therefore quicker to download into a web page.

MARC

Machine Readable Cataloging. "The MARC formats are standards for the representation and communication of bibliographic and related information in machine readable form." The MARC formats contain an explicit set of rules for the structure of fields and the content values within those fields. More information about MARC is available at http://lcweb.loc.gov/marc/

Metadata

Data about data, or information known about the image in order to provide access to the image. Usually includes information about the intellectual content of the image, digital representation data, and security or rights management information.

Migration

Preserving the integrity of digital images by transferring them across hardware and software configurations and across subsequent generations of computer technology. Migration includes refreshment (copying digital files from one media to another) as a means of preservation and access. However, migration differs from refreshment in the sense that it is not always possible to make an exact copy of a database or even an image file as changes in hardware and software occur and still maintain compatibility with the new generation of technology.

Noise

Data or unidentifiable marks picked up in the course of scanning or data transfer that do not correspond to the original.

Pixel

Often referred to as dot, as in "dots per inch." "Pixel" is short for picture elements, which make up an image, similar to grains in a photograph or dots in a half-tone. Each pixel can represent a number of different shades or colors, depending on how much storage space is allocated for it. Pixels per inch (ppi) is sometimes the preferred term, as it more accurately describes the digital image.

Preservation

(As it relates to scanning) Digitizing an original photograph, document, or three-dimensional object is only a method of preservation if the digital file becomes the access tool and the original is no longer available for use. Although high resolution scanning (i.e., scan at the highest resolution possible appropriate to the type of media you are scanning) is recommended for all materials in order to achieve the highest quality possible and to ensure that information held in the original is not lost in the scan. However, the digital file, as of yet, should not serve as a replacement of the original for preservation purposes.

Quality Control

Techniques ensuring that high quality is maintained through various stages of a process. For example, quality control during image capture might include comparing the scanned image to the original and then adjusting colors or tonal values, or checking for artifacts.

Refreshment

The transfer of digital files to a new media on a regular basis. This is the most important part of an institution's long-term commitment to digitization. Technology is usually outdated by the time it hits the marketplace. The data we generate today must be retrievable five, fifty, and a hundred years from now. In order to ensure long-term access to the data, it must be transferred to the most recent and stable type of media storage. In a hundred years, it is very unlikely that any of the computers on our desks today will function. We must make sure that the data can be retrieved by future technology.

Resolution

The number of pixels (in both height and width) making up an image. The more pixels in an image, the higher the resolution, and the higher the resolution of an image, the greater its clarity and definition (and the larger the file size). Resolution can also refer to the output device, such as a computer monitor or printer, used to display the image. Image file resolution is often expressed as a ratio (such as 640x480 pixels), as is monitor resolution; however, resolution is also expressed in terms of dots per inch (dpi). The asssumed universal monitor resolution for web users is 72 dpi. Image file resolution and output (print or display) resolution combine to influence the clarity of a digital image when it is viewed.

Scanner

A device for capturing a digital image. There are many types of scanners, such as flatbed scanners, drum scanners, slide scanners, and microfilm scanners.

Scanning

see Image Capture

SGML

Standard Generalized Markup Language. An international standard for the definition of device-independent, system-independent methods of representing texts in electronic form. SGML emphasizes descriptive rather than procedural markup. While HTML is a markup language which deals primarily with the appearance of a document, SGML is a more complex system for describing structural divisions in a text (title page, chapter, scene, stanza), typographical elements (changing typefaces), and other textual features (grammatical structure, etc.). The "tags" in SGML preserve the structure of a text, enable the user to constrain

searches to particular structural features of the text and aid in the navigation and use of the text. More information on SGML is available at
http://sunsite.berkeley.edu/SGML/

Subsampling
Using an algorithm to derive a lower-resolution image from a higher-
resolution image.

Surrogate image
A representation of the original image, used for study.

TEI
Text Encoding Initiative. An international project to develop guidelines
for the preparation and exchange of electronic texts for scholarly research. The TEI has created a set of SGML DTDs for the encoding of
humanities and social science-related texts. More information on TEI is
available at http://etext.virginia.edu/TEI.html

TIFF
Tagged Image/Interchange File Format. A file storage format implemented on a wide variety of computer systems, usually used for archival scans.

URL
Uniform Resource Locator. A standard addressing scheme used to locate
or reference files on the Internet. Used in World Wide Web documents to
locate files. A URL gives the type of resource being used and the path to
the file. The syntax used is: scheme://host.domain/path filename.

URN
Universal Resource Name/Number. A storage-independent scheme to
name all resources on the Internet with a unique and fixed name. URNs
are likely to supersede URLs for identification and referencing of net-
worked resources.

World Wide Web (WWW)
An interconnected network of electronic hypermedia documents available on the Internet. WWW documents are marked up in HTML. Cross
references or hyperlinks between documents are recorded in the form of
URLs.

XML
Extensible Markup Language. Designed to enable the use of SGML on
the World Wide Web. XML is a metalanguage (a way to define tag sets)
that allows you to design your own customized markup language for
many classes of documents. XML is designed for easy and straightforward use of SGML on the web, ease of use in authoring and managing
SGML documents, and ease of transmission and sharing of electronic
documents across the web. XML is intended to deliver information, not
just pages. XML preserves the key ideas of SGML, only simplifies them.

Zooming
Enlarging a portion of a digital image in order to see it more clearly or make it easier to alter.

Definitions taken from The Nebraska State Historical Society Glossary of Digital Imaging Terms and "A Glossary of Scanning Terms" from *Preservation Resources*.

The Digital Libraries Initiative Glossary can be found at http://dli.grainger.uiuc.edu/glossary.htm

Appendix C

QUICK TIPS TO MAKE ACCESSIBLE WEB SITES

For Complete Guidelines & Checklist: www.w3.org/WAI

- **Images & animations:** Use the **alt** attribute to describe the function of each visual.

- **Image maps.** Use the client-side **map** and text for hotspots.

- **Multimedia.** Provide captioning and transcripts of audio, and descriptions of video.

- **Hypertext links.** Use text that makes sense when read out of context. For example, avoid "click here."

- **Page organization.** Use headings, lists, and consistent structure. Use **CSS** for layout and style where possible.

- **Graphs & charts.** Summarize or use the **longdesc** attribute.

- **Scripts, applets, & plug-ins.** Provide alternative content in case active features are inaccessible or unsupported.

- **Frames.** Use the **noframes** element and meaningful titles.

- **Tables.** Make line-by-line reading sensible. Summarize.

- **Check your work.** Validate. Use tools, checklist, and guidelines at http://www.w3.org/TR/WCAG

Bibliography

Besser, Howard and Trant, Jennifer. *Introduction to Imaging: issues in constructing an image database.* Santa Monica, CA: The Getty Art History Information Program, 1995.

Digitization Glossary. 2003. Collaborative Digitization Program. http://www. http://www.cdpheritage.org/digital/glossary.cfm

Kalfatovic, Martin. *Creating a Winning Online Exhibition: A Guide for Libraries, Archives, and Museums.* Chicago: American Library Association, 2002.

Koelling, Jill Marie. *Digital Imaging: a practical approach.* Walnut Creek, CA: AltaMira Press, 2004.

Leab Exhibition Awards Evaluation Criteria. 2003. Rare Books and Manuscripts Section, American Library Association. http://www.rbms.nd.edu/committees/exhibition_awards/

McFarland, David Sawyer. *Dreamweaver MX 2004: The Missing Manual.* Sebastopol, CA: Pogue Press/O'Reilly & Associates, Inc., 2003.

Meyer, Eric A. *Cascading Style Sheets: The Definitive Guide.* Sebastapol, CA: O'Reilly, 2000.

Nielsen, Jakob and Tahir, Marie. *Homepage Usability: 50 websites deconstructed.* New Riders Publishing, 2002.

Rosenfeld, Louis and Morville, Peter. *Information Architecture for the World Wide Web.* Cambridge, MA: O'Reilly, 2002.

TASI: Technical Advisory Service for Images. http://www.tasi.ac.uk/

Towers, J. Tarin. *Macromedia Dreamweaver MX 2004 for Windows and MacIntosh.* Berkeley: Peachpit Press, 2005.

Western States Imaging Best Practices. 2003. Collaborative Digitization Program. http://www.cdpheritage.org/westerntrails/wt_bpscanning.html

World Wide Web Consortium, WAI Accessibility Initiative: Quick Tips to Make Accessible Web Sites. 2005.
http://www.w3.org/WAI/References/QuickTips/

All exhibition illustrations courtesy of the Spencer Research Library, University of Kansas, Lawrence, Kansas.

All *Young American Readers* images are drawn from the Charles and E. Jennifer Monaghan Collection at the Spencer Research Library.

Index

About the Author

Sarah Goodwin Thiel is the Digital Imaging Librarian at the University of Kansas. She holds a Master of Arts in Library Science from the University of Missouri, Columbia and a Bachelor of Arts with a specialization in studio art from Southern Illinois University, Edwardsville. Sarah serves as the imaging specialist for a wide spectrum of digital projects underway at the University of Kansas and produces instruction programs to assist faculty in the development of digital materials. Prior to her current appointment, she served as the Digital Projects Librarian at the Spencer Research Library, the university's rare books and manuscripts library. In that role, she designed and created digital versions of many of the major and minor exhibitions mounted in the library. Sarah is active in the digital imaging profession and specializes in the digitization of special collections materials. She is a member of the Rare Books and Manuscripts Section (RBMS) Exhibition Awards Committee and presents regularly on topics relating to digitization, collaboration, and access to collections.

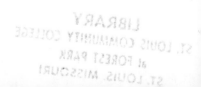